CRE▲TIVE
HOMEOWNER®

WHAT NOT TO BUILD

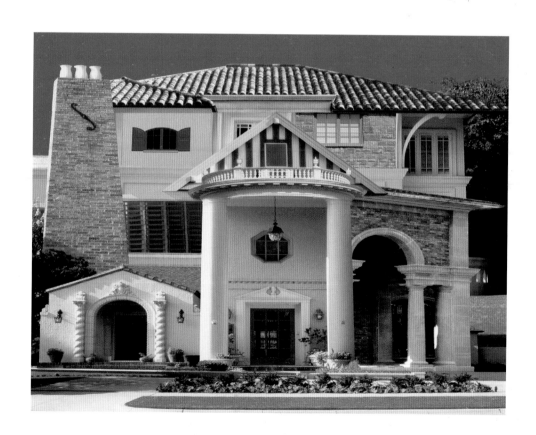

CREATIVE
HOMEOWNER®

WHAT NOT TO BUILD

ARCHITECTURAL OPTIONS FOR HOMEOWNERS

SANDRA EDELMAN ▪ JUDY GAMAN ▪ ROBBY REID, R.A.

CREATIVE HOMEOWNER®, Upper Saddle River, New Jersey

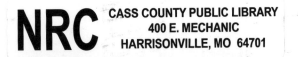

What Not to Build
MANAGING EDITOR: Fran J. Donegan
ASSISTANT EDITOR: Evan Lambert
EDITORIAL INTERN: Jennifer Calvert
INDEXER: Schroeder Indexing Services
LAYOUT AND DESIGN: Natalie Salvucci, 3r1 Group
PHOTO MANIPULATION: Clarke Barre
COVER IMAGE: Ben Britt

Creative Homeowner
PRESIDENT: Brian Toolan
VP/EDITORIAL DIRECTOR: Timothy O. Bakke
PRODUCTION MANAGER: Kimberly H. Vivas
MANAGING EDITOR: Fran J. Donegan
ART DIRECTOR: David Geer

Printed in China

Current Printing (last digit)
10 9 8 7 6 5 4 3 2
What Not To Build, First Edition
Library of Congress Control Number: 2005931076

ISBN-10: 1-58011-293-5
ISBN-13: 978-1-58011-293-2

Creative Homeowner®
A Division of Federal Marketing Corp.
24 Park Way, Upper Saddle River, NJ 07458
www.creativehomeowner.com

Acknowledgements

We want to thank all of the people at Creative Homeowner who worked on the book, including Fran Donegan, our editor, for his humor and ability to modify architectural jargon into understandable terms. Thanks to Tim Bakke for his initial interest and assigning us Clarke Barre, a unique artist whose belief in the subject is evidenced by the late night e-mails and the inclusion of the "Architects Notebook."

Our photographer Dan Piassick deserves a medal for his patience. He never grumbled when asked to photograph "just one more house" in the hot Texas sun. Special thanks to him for riding around in his truck with Sandy all those months and his willingness to backtrack for that perfect oversized dormer or undersized entry that were passed a few blocks back.

Behind the scenes, we want to thank 3r1 Design Group, all the homeowners who allowed us to photograph their homes, Ben Britt, whose image on the cover planted the seed for this book almost 10 years ago, George Pelletier for his complete support and belief in the project, Thomas Fitzwilliam for his input in the landscape chapter, and finally Dean Smith for his help with the 360 chapter.

Our greatest thanks is reserved for our families whose unwavering support had them taking a back seat as they sacrificed their time for all the hours we spent working on the book.

Contents

Introduction

This book is about the houses we drive by every day, and its goal is to assist the people who design, build, and buy them. For whatever reason, many modern homes incorporate incorrect design elements that appear out of place, usually affecting the street elevation of the house in a negative manner. Simply visit most neighborhoods—especially those built within the last 20 years—and you will recognize that many houses need help. This dilemma is multiplied significantly when you consider that many of today's homes are mass-produced for large subdivisions. This is not to suggest that these residences are totally deficient aesthetically. They are not. In fact, many houses simply require cosmetic corrections.

To the average homeowner, identifying design errors may be intuitive. Most people can express that they don't like something, although they may not be able to state exactly what about the design they don't like. In addition, people usually have a difficult time explaining why they think something is well done. *What Not*

Most people have an intuitive sense when something is well designed.

Good design solves the problems posed by the constraints of a building site.

To Build gives readers the information they need to articulate their opinions. The book contains real houses with real problems and the solutions to make them better. By examining accepted design principles and showing how they relate to many of the homes being built today, we as residential designers, architects, and home-buyers can help improve the overall design of houses.

In architecture, design responds to existing conditions. These constraints may be functional or a composite of monetary and jurisdictional encumbrances, such as building codes and zoning ordinances. The design of a building must resolve these constraints. In residential design and construction, "the problem" may be a result of the introduction of "production housing," which started in the 1950s in Levittown, New York. For our purposes, the most significant aspect of this occurrence was that single-family housing became based on a mass-market philosophy.

Prior to this milestone, historical perspective influenced home design. Whether it was a mansion or a modest folk home, a European influence was evident in its design. Why is this significant? Up to that point in time, architects designed the majority of residences or residential builders who were a product of schools or guilds emulated popular designs. Any architect of that time was a product of an education deeply immersed in the definition of classical styles. As such, interpretation of the various genres into regional styles evolved into the "retro" styles of their day or expressions we currently call Neo-Classical, Greek Revival, etc.

Today, most homes are not designed by architects. Although it would be easy to say that the problem, which we've defined as poor design due to an ineffectual application of design principles, could be solved by having all houses designed by architects, that is not the point. Our underlying goal is to share with our readers those fundamental architectural premises that will enable them, whether they are a homeowner, designer, or contractor, to create a final design that is aesthetically pleasing, grounded in the tenants of good design, and has mass-market appeal. Essentially, we want to create a "visual literacy," which can be applied by anyone who follows the guidelines written in this book.

The intent is for the reader to use this sourcebook as a reference. Terms such as scale, proportion, balance, rhythm, and composition are introduced. These concepts are explained and then elaborated upon in the various chapters. Each chapter concentrates on a particular element of the house, such as porches, windows, or columns. There are also chapters on using proportion and balance in design, selecting materials, ornamentation, and landscaping. The focus is on how the individual pieces can be composed using the basic organizing design principles. In essence, these examples give the reader a visual context of the vocabulary that is the language of design.

We have limited this edition to single-family homes with a variety of price ranges. The solutions depicted have minimal impact on the floor plan or functional aspects of the house. This highlights our opinion that most design miscues can be corrected through the application of design principles and reinforces the notion that good design is not a function of spending excessive amounts of money. In many cases, there will be a cost reduction in new construction.

Ultimately, our goal is that a person who has no prior experience or education in design or architecture can study this book and become familiar with the basic rules of scale, proportion, balance, etc. Applying these concepts to any project will aid in achieving a final design that will stand the test of time. The purpose of this book is to arm the reader with a basic vocabulary in design, which will, in turn, create the confidence to apply the fundamental elements

This is an example of establishing rhythm in architecture.

Material selection is an important component of good design.

Adhering to design principles does not sacrifice individuality.

and principles to create better housing. The intent is also to assist multiple users in addressing design miscues, whether it is the homeowner who is purchasing with an intent to remodel, the homeowner who already owns and wants to remedy inefficiencies in their residence, residential designers who may or may not be cognizant of appropriate design criteria, home builders who are well versed in construction techniques but are limited in design expertise, or architects who may be unfamiliar with the application of known design principles in the residential milieu.

The greatest financial purchase most people will make portrays an individual identity and makes a statement about who is behind the front door. Good design is not a function of money; in fact many of our suggested solutions would cost less if they had been constructed with the correct architectural principles. It is our hope that the reader will be able to employ or direct others to implement the design strategies elaborated in this book to achieve a fundamentally sound, aesthetically pleasing, and economically efficient residence that contributes to the context of the community.

Landscape design contributes to the overall impression of a house.

Principles of Design

Why the Past Matters

Many people believe that older homes tend to be more charming and have more character than most of the houses built today. What defines charming? What is this quality that captivates us and makes these homes so inviting? What makes older neighborhoods so appealing? Maybe it's because the houses in older neighborhoods usually incorporated classic design techniques more often than many houses being built today. Good design just "feels" right, and that is what we respond to.

This feeling is the unconscious response to the correct application of architectural principles. Understanding and using the fundamental principles of *mass, balance, scale, proportion,* and *rhythm* will help you create timeless residential designs and beautiful neighborhoods.

Thomas Jefferson, although not an architect, constructed one of the most famous homes in American history. Monticello, which means "little mountain" in Italian, was inspired by the architect Andrea Palladio (1508-1580) who was known for his mastery of

The designer of this house used some of the same design principles Thomas Jefferson used to create Monticello.

proportion and scale. The 21-room residence was completed in 1809 and has Roman, Palladian, and French details that still influence American architecture today.

Monticello incorporated many of the architectural principles that create an aesthetically pleasing design. For example, the entry element—columns, beam, and pediment—is in scale with the rest of the elevation. The use of the pediment and portico is a technique that downsizes the primary mass of the main house behind it. The columns are proportionally correct in reference to the beam above. Behind the columns, the windows and doors create a human scale as you enter the home. These elements combine to form a symmetrically balanced elevation.

Monticello combines Roman, French, and Palladian architectural details in its design.

Lessons from Jefferson

As with Monticello, the modern day house shown opposite applies the principles to create a design that is aesthetically pleasing. The projected gabled entry is in scale with the elevation behind it, as is the column-supported portico of Monticello. The entry surround and window above also create a human scale at the front door. If you drew a line through the center of the elevation, you would see a perfectly symmetrically balanced home. The dormers, in tandem with the gabled entry, create a rhythm that ascends in height at the center. Proportion, mass, scale, balance, and rhythm may sound like technical terms, but as you can see, applying them correctly is rewarding.

Learning the Basics

The purpose of this book is to help architects, builders, and homebuyers apply the principles of good design to the houses they build and renovate, and to the homes they buy. Unfortunately, most people are rarely exposed to examples of good architecture because many homes are built without incorporating good design principles. This book will help you apply these age-old principles to new and existing residential construction. We will show real houses that need to be fixed and how to fix them.

Design Principle: Mass

Mass is the bulk or the largest portion of the home. As individual pieces, mass becomes interesting when you create combinations of these shapes, much like children's building blocks. The arrangement of these geometric shapes (square, rectangle, circle, etc.) to create "weight" is called massing. The designer arranges these large elements into a combination that is aesthetically pleasing. As the shapes are combined, they are divided into categories, such as primary and secondary mass.

The *primary mass* is the largest shape in the building block. The *secondary masses* represent the additional shapes that are added to create the overall look of the home. Windows, doors, and open spaces are *voids* that create negative space and allow for breaks within masses.

A knowledgeable architect or builder will carefully arrange the masses and the voids. It's important that the secondary masses don't compete with the primary mass. A projected entry—which is a secondary mass—that is too large will overwhelm the house—the primary mass—behind it. Placing voids that allow for natural breaks in the masses create balance and rhythm across the elevation.

The primary mass shown here is the largest shape in the building block. The secondary mass is in balance with the primary mass behind it.

Design Principle: Balance

Balance is the visual relationship among the parts of a house on either side of an imaginary centerline drawn through the house. When a house is well balanced, there is a state of equilibrium between these contrasting elements. The arrangement, the size, and the shapes of these parts determines whether or not a house is visually balanced. Balance is usually described as symmetrical or asymmetrical.

In a symmetrically balanced house, the shapes on one side of the centerline match the shapes on the opposite side—creating two visually equal halves. In an asymmetrically balanced house, the shapes do not match exactly, but if the shapes have equal visual weight, they are visually balanced.

The mirror images on either side of the centerline create symmetrical balance.

Asymmetrical balance is achieved by placing different shapes with visually equal weight on either side of an imaginary centerline.

Design Principle: Scale

In architecture, scale refers to the size of something compared to a reference standard, or how we perceive the size of something in relation to something else. For example, construction drawings, or blueprints, use a scale of 1 inch to 1 foot. So a building that is 30 feet long would be shown in scale as 30 inches long. This allows the building to be represented on a sheet of paper.

One tool for measuring scale is the human body. The human being as the basic unit of measurement has been used for a long time. The Vitruvian Man, a famous drawing by Leonardo da Vinci, is often used to illustrate this concept. Historically, it was thought if God created man, the planet's highest form of life, then harmony could be achieved by using the human body as the basic measurement for a comparative scale. An 8-foot ceiling can feel cozy and homelike, while a soaring ceiling in a cathedral draws our eye upward and creates a space of reverence. The scale of something in relation to us will affect our perception of its size.

Note the relationship of the tree to the house in these illustrations. The scale of an object in relation to another object will affect our perception of the object's size.

Design Principle: Proportion

Proportion is related to both size and balance, and visually refers to the proper relationships of one part to another or to the whole. Renaissance architects believed that architecture was mathematics translated into spatial units. Many acceptable standards used today reflect the Greek system of proportion. Just as the human body influenced scale, proportion has its roots in mathematics.

Pythagoras (569 BC-475 BC) discovered that the Greek musical system could be expressed by a numerical progression. Later, Plato elaborated on this theory to develop aesthetics of proportion. Today, rectangles using the proportions of 2:3, 3:5, and 5:8 are considered very pleasing. To translate those proportions into feet, if each unit equaled one foot, then a 2:3 ratio would be a rectangle that measures 2 feet by 3 feet. If each unit were 2 feet, then a 2:3 ratio would be a rectangle that measures 4 feet by 6 feet.

Andrea Palladio, most often recognized today for Palladian windows, published *The Four Books on Architecture* in 1570 and described the seven "most beautiful and proportional manner of rooms." Once again, you'll see the ratios of 2:3, 3:5, and 1:2.

In residential design, the purpose of a proportional system is to help establish a visual relationship between all parts of an exterior elevation. By doing so, a sense of harmony and order can be achieved. Although materials, options, and the styles of houses change, correct proportions are timeless.

As twenty-first century homeowners, we have the luxury of selecting pieces off the shelf to build our homes. Most exterior building materials use standard ratios that have aesthetically pleasing proportions—many based on the Greek Golden Mean. (See "What the Golden Mean Means to You," page 21.) All we have to do is concentrate on combining those proportionally to the entire facade.

Rectangles in various proportions are used in this home's elevation. These shapes, along with the relationship between the gable end and the porch, and the upper roof to the second-floor wall, combine to form a harmonious front elevation.

DESIGN 101

Proportion Matters

"Hence no building can be said to be well designed which wants symmetry and proportion. In truth they are as necessary to the beauty of a building as to that of a well-formed human figure..."
—Vitruvius, Book III, Chap. 1

Marcus Vitruvius Pollio, a Roman architect (30 BC – 46 AD), developed his ideas of architecture based on the proportions of the human body. Later, Leonardo da Vinci drew the Vitruvian Man as his interpretation of those ideas.

The perfectly proportioned human body is pleasing to the eye. Likewise, architecture that is carefully constructed using the same ratios is intuitively pleasing. The answer lies in mathematical ratios that were discovered thousands of years ago by using the human figure as a model.

Before building or remodeling your home, look for proportional patterns. This can be done with grid overlays or the simple use of tools, such as a ruler and compass.

Here is the ideally proportioned man.

- The eyes are halfway between the top of the head and the chin.

- The corners of the mouth line up with the centers of the eyes.

- The width from shoulder to shoulder is 3 heads width.

- The distance from the wrist to the end of the outstretched fingers of the hand is 1 head.

- The distance from the elbow to the end of outstretched fingers is 2 heads.

- Outstretched arms, finger tip to finger tip, is the same measurement as a persons height.

- The foot is the same length as the distance from the elbow to the wrist

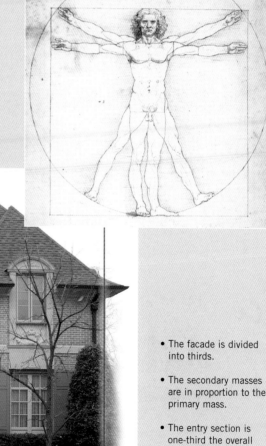

- The facade is divided into thirds.

- The secondary masses are in proportion to the primary mass.

- The entry section is one-third the overall house width.

- The second story is in proportion to the ground level.

- The house is symmetrically balanced.

1/3   1/3   1/3

Design Principle: Rhythm

Rhythm, usually associated with music, is a repetitive element often used in design. It organizes forms and leads the viewer's eyes— think of columns or a series of arches. Repetition of a design or a building part usually expresses movement or animation. A row of dormers, sequence of windows, or repetitive rooflines are examples of rhythm in architecture.

Like patterns found in nature, rhythm establishes predictability in design. Viewers expect to see more of certain elements, and with good residential design they will. If you see one arch, you expect to see another; if one column is present, more should follow.

In the following chapters, the focus will be on common mistakes made in residential design. All of these mistakes are the result of a failure to apply an architectural principle. When a house is aesthetically pleasing, the designer has understood these principles.

The columns are a repetitive element and seem to march along the porch.

It's All in Your Mind

Every time we look at our environment, we try to make sense of what we see. Psychological theories have verified that the mind will simplify the visual environment in order to understand it. Gestalt psychologists from the 1920s and 1930s described and identified the natural units of perceptions and how we observe them. These discoveries are important to remember when applying the fundamental principles of architecture. Principles of proximity and similarity explain how the mind works in the visual interpretation of shapes, textures, and objects, and why the incorrect arrangements of these create visual clutter. Given any composition of forms, we tend to reduce the subject to the simplest and most regular shapes. This concept is the most important idea to remember in applying the fundamental principles and understanding why they are so effective.

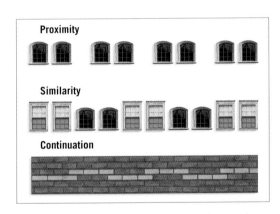

The Principle of Proximity states that objects that are close together, or in the same visual field, should complement one another. It is disturbing if they don't. Our eyes tend to group items together. For example, these windows will be viewed as four sets of two, rather than eight individual windows.

The Principle of Similarity explains how the eye is easily able to move over objects that share common textures or colors. Too many textures or colors cause a disruption. That is why when you look at a house that is cluttered and busy, you wish to look away. Clutter, defined as too many shapes, too much variety, or general disorganization of materials, creates visual chaos. We view the windows in groups of similarity.

The Principle of Continuation describes how the eye will move along a path in a given direction to a final point. Through continuation, rhythm in architecture establishes a sense of order. It is a useful tool in creating movement that leads the eye across an elevation to a focal point. Although the pattern of the bricks is exactly the same, the different color helps our eye navigate from one end of the design to the other.

DESIGN 101

What the Golden Mean Means to You

The ancient Greeks sought out perfect proportions for architecture. They looked to geometrical patterns and found that they could be replicated in the construction of buildings to give strength and beauty. The Parthenon, a building most people have heard of, was built using these proportions.

The Greek discoveries about proportion are fascinating because they echo those proportions that are often found in nature.

Create Perfection 1. Draw a square, and place a dot in the middle of the bottom line as we have done here. **2.** Place the pivot of a compass on the dot, and extend the compass to the upper corner of the square. Draw an outer arc, stopping level with the initial bottom line. **3.** Then use the endpoint of the arc as the corner to form new lines. Now you have a perfect rectangle!

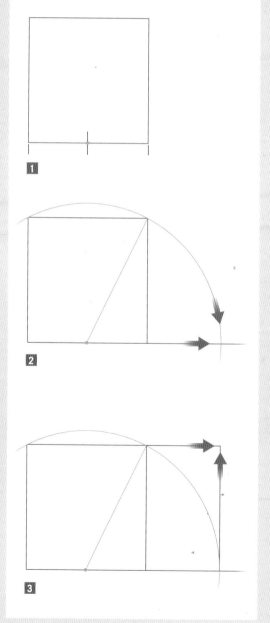

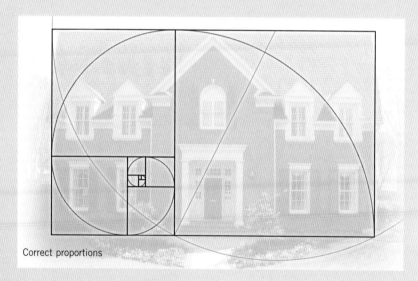

Correct proportions

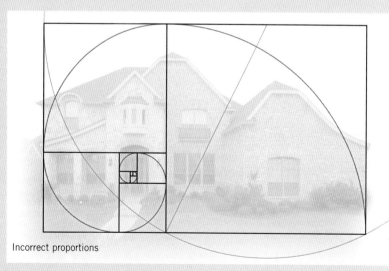

Incorrect proportions

What does this have to do with houses? Following the rules of proportion will help create an outside elevation that is visually pleasing. On the contrary, failure to do so will result in an elevation that is erratic or unbalanced.

CHAPTER 2

The Front Entry

The Place to Begin

People begin forming opinions of the inside of your home as soon as they see the front elevation. The minds of first-time visitors may cycle through a variety of impressions as they make their way from the front walk or driveway to the front entry. What visitors see outside is what they expect to find inside your home—that's why the front entry is so important.

There are three types of entries: recessed, flush, and projected. The *recessed* entrance creates an outdoor foyer that serves as a transition between the outdoors and the interior spaces. A *flush* entrance lines up with the exterior wall of the house, using trimwork, surrounds, and sidelights to bring attention to the entry. A *projected* entrance extends forward to greet visitors. The projection may be nothing more than a simple overhang that provides shelter from the elements and is supported by brackets or columns. Or it can be a totally covered area.

A well-designed entry is critical to the design success of your home. The size and placement of the entry is used to help balance other components of the facade. The main entry door is an important element in front entry design and should focus the attention of those passing by. Other elements of good entry design include

- The entry door should not be confused with other doors on the front elevation.

- Materials used in the entry should complement those used in the primary mass of the home.

- The approach to the entrance should be inviting.

- The use of landscaping should help direct visitors to the front door.

- Transoms used above the door should never be larger than the door itself.

- Sidelights should be no wider than half the width of the door.

✓ What to Build

The stone path, low walls, courtyard, and whimsical entry overhang enhance the sense of arrival at this storybook home.

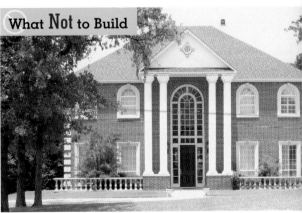

⃠ What **Not** to Build

This monumental-sized entry is more appropriate to a cathedral than a human-scaled house. The oversized transom above the door is almost double the height of the front door and is out of scale. The columns on either side visually amplify the problem.

What to Build

Here is an example of how a standard-size door stands out on a large facade. The distinctive color forces passersby to focus on the entry, and it displays the owner's individuality.

What Not to Build

The equal emphasis and ornamentation of the pair of arches fails to decisively signify "entry" and causes visual confusion.

The Disappearing Entry

This barely perceptible projected entry is far too small for the front facade of this house. The large secondary mass beside it overpowers the front door to the point that it takes a second to locate the door from the street. The entry area is sheathed in siding, which, due to its limited amount, makes it feel even more undersized. Its roof is so shallow that it disappears. The narrow walkway constricts the entry experience, making it less inviting.

The secondary mass towers over the doorway.

✓ Add a custom door to make the entry stand out.

The shed roof disappears into the main roof.

✓ Extend the gable roofline to integrate the doorway with the secondary mass.

What **Not** to Build

The narrow walkway creates a tunnel effect on the approach to the door.

✓ Widen the walkway and steps to make the entry more inviting.

The change of material creates an entry element that is too small for the facade.

✓ Simplify the materials palette. Use brick to unify the entire section.

✓ What to Build

The way to correct this entry is to integrate it into the secondary mass beside it. Incorporate the entry into the large gable-end section. Use brick as the unifying element, and change the slope of the roofline. These changes create a correctly scaled entry in the balanced elevation. Widening the walkway emphasizes the prominence of the entry and makes it more inviting.

Architect's Notebook

DELETE SIDING SHOW BRICK

CREATE NEW ROOF LINE.

EXTEND ROOF LINE

CUSTOM DOOR

USE OF BRICK SIMPLIFIES MATERIAL PALETTE

SHOW WOOD DOOR

WIDER WALKWAY STEPS ARE MORE INVITING.

OLD WALL LINE

WIDEN ENTRY

DESIGN 101

Understanding Entry Types

Flush Entry

A flush entry is on the same plane as the front wall. The use of a pediment and trim details that are in keeping with the style of the house, along with the introduction of a bold or contrasting color for the door, helps distinguish the entry from the rest of the facade.

Recessed Entry

A recessed entry is located behind the main frontal wall plane of a house. In this symmetrically balanced home, the entry divides the facade in two and creates an outdoor foyer.

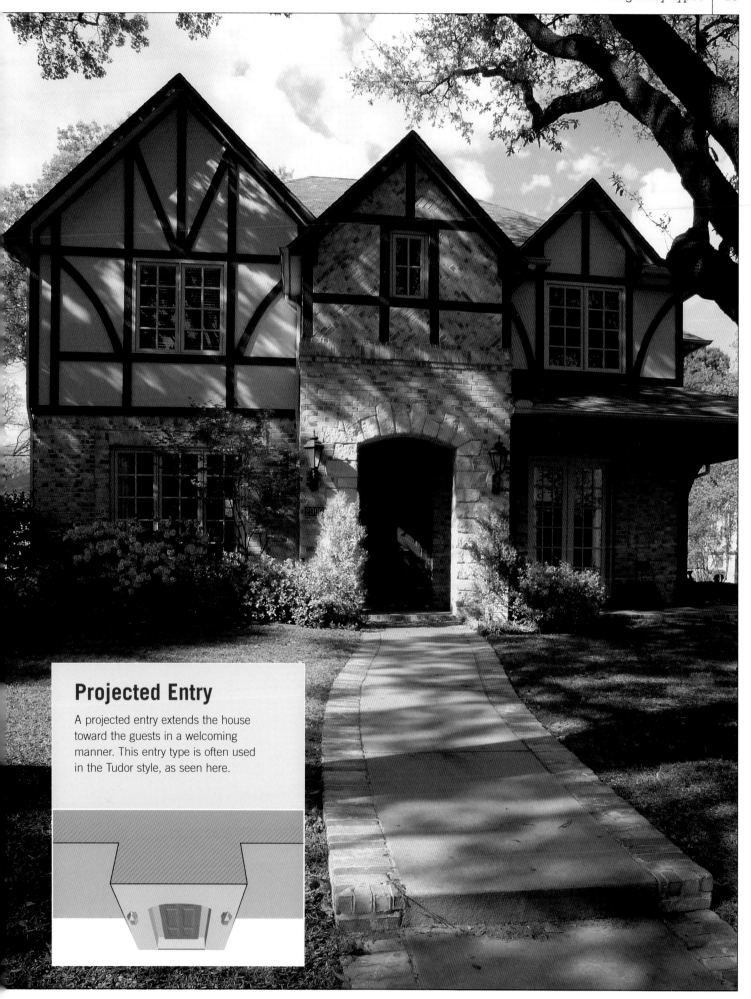

Projected Entry

A projected entry extends the house toward the guests in a welcoming manner. This entry type is often used in the Tudor style, as seen here.

Where's the Door?

This two-story entry uses columns to frame the front door with the purpose of creating a focal point. These ornamental pillars are the main design feature, but in this case they fall short of their intended goals. The lack of a beam, or entablature, which acts as a termination point, allows the eye to continue upward, resulting in an elongated appearance. In addition, the pillars appear merely ornamental, with no structural reason for their use. The exaggerated height of the columns is out of scale and causes the standard-size front door to look too small. The large window above it further overpowers the door.

The fanlight window causes confusion because this type is normally used as a transom.

✓ Add the correct window style and scale to complement other entry features.

What **Not** to Build

The eye keeps moving upward due to the lack of a terminating beam.

✓ Remove the columns to declutter the front facade.

The height of the columns dwarfs the front door.

✓ Add a double door with sidelights and transom to create the correct scale.

✓ What to Build

To achieve the correct proportions, remove the columns—this will also give a less-cluttered-looking appearance to the front facade—and make the front door larger and the second-story window smaller. Replace the front door. The door, sidelights, and fanlight shown here are well integrated and work with the style of home. These changes return the design emphasis to the entry and reinforce its prominence.

DESIGN101

Supersized:
Bigger is not always better

Large entry areas are usually used to draw attention to a house. Designers of churches and government buildings employ this technique to make the building more prominent. However, this entry is exaggerated and out of scale with the rest of the house, and the columns create the illusion that the large stone arch is floating above the entry. The contrasting materials chosen for the archway only add to the problem by drawing attention to this flawed detail. The arch is too large, and the double columns are not correctly placed. The columns should rest solidly under the arch, but this arch looks as though it is in danger of toppling over. The collection of windows at the entry appears to be an attempt to fill up the space, but the real problem is the over-scaled archway, which magnifies the void.

Cut the Clutter

This is an excellent example of a rampant design philosophy that assumes that placing interesting objects in front of, around, and on top of an entry achieves emphasis and focus.

The use of four materials — stone, brick trim, concrete columns, and wood overhang — creates design confusion.

✓ Simplify the materials pallet by removing the arched entry.

What **Not** to Build

The column material is out of place with the brick and country styling of the house.

✓ Replace the white columns with wood posts to unify the entry elements.

The entry appears tacked on to the house. It is not integrated into the secondary mass.

✓ Add a tall pergola under the overhang. The pergola creates entry hierarchy and repeats the horizontal line established by the existing pergolas.

✓ What to **Build**

Changing the columns and the overhang creates a pleasing appearance and unifies the entry elements. It is interesting that the elements that were removed were replaced. The difference is that the new components—the main pergola and wood posts—better suit the design of the house and hence give the facade a cleaner, less-cluttered appearance.

DESIGN 101

Incompatible Materials

There are too many elements used at this entrance. The lines in the entry surround conflict with the ornate patterns in the glass and iron door. The entry appears tacked on and is out of context with the balance of the elevation.

DESIGN 101

Entries Done Right

The importance of the entry to the overall design of the home is evident in the five examples shown here. In all cases, the entry area is used in the design to provide balance to the front facade of the house. All of the entries are focal points, although each has a unique design method to gain attention.

A Balanced Approach

This recessed entry is integrated into the wall plane to form a large element that balances the front elevation in relation to the roof mass beyond. The gable-end projection adjacent to the arched opening reduces the scale of the entry element in the same manner that the dormers reduce the remaining roof mass. The double dormers, gables, windows, and wall vents combine to create a pleasing design.

- The use of matching material and roof forms, or shapes, creates an understated entry element.
- Integrating the covered entry into the vertical wall plane achieves a recessed design.
- A walkway and full-width steps help make the front door a destination.

Details Make the Difference

Balance does not need to be boring. Here is an example of a projected entry that uses rhythm and bold details to create a unique and contemporary entrance that is true to the architectural style of the house. Note how the pitch of the entry roof matches that of the dormers and large gable.

- The gable-end entry repeats the main roof forms to create rhythm.
- The bold trim and semicircular element create a unique entry that is harmonious to the overall design.
- The columns support a roof to form a projected entry.

Balancing Act

This is a symmetrically balanced home with a flush entry as its center element. The stone door surround, which starts at the ground plane, ties into the roof above and provides a prominent two-story entry feature. The radiating front steps and vertical plantings accentuate the design hierarchy.

- Distinctive stone trim from ground to roof emphasizes the importance of the entrance.

- The ornate door offers a visual clue to the homeowner's outlook on the transition from public to private space.

The Traditional Approach

This flush entrance creates the centerline on which the main portion of the facade is symmetrically balanced. The use of color and ornamentation eliminates any doubt as to the entrance of the home.

- The entry placement creates the centerline for a symmetrically balanced facade.

- The door trim, although traditional in design, is distinctive enough to differentiate the door opening in the wall plane.

- Bright color creates a focal point and expresses individuality.

Sublime Symmetry

The entry element is scaled to portray the importance of the front door and is symmetrically designed to balance the elevation. The full-width walkway and plantings contribute to the overall effect.

- Columns and a rectangular pediment form an implied surround, enhancing the hierarchy of the front door.

- The entry element is symmetrical and balances the front facade.

- The door surround is typical of a flush entry.

A Top-Heavy Facade

This photo demonstrates how the scale of a design component can be disproportionate to the balance of an elevation. The entry feature creates a secondary mass that is oversized in relation to the overall design. The material used for the upper balcony creates an illusion of weight that conflicts with the slender columns below. Visually, the upper element is too large for the mass behind it and the supports below. The intent is to draw the eye to the front door; instead, the massive element is so out of place that it becomes a distraction from the symmetrically balanced home.

Add quoins to match others on the house.

What Not to Build

The entry feature is oversized in relation to the front door and overall design.

Removing the oversized entry feature and extending the balcony creates a balanced elevation.

This window is the wrong size and style for a balcony setting.

Add French Doors to complete the balcony.

✓ What to **Build**

Removing the top portion of the entry and extending the balcony change the scale and correct the elevation. Note how the front of the balcony is in proportion to the columns. It contains the ornament used on the original house and quoins that match those on the corners of the house. Also, the large center window is converted to French doors to match those on the first floor.

Architect's Notebook

REMOVE ENTRY DORMER

ADD WALL LIGHTS

USE THE TALLER BALUSTRADE FOR RAILING

RAISE COLUMN TO THIS LINE

QUOINS

An Out-of-Proportion Entry

The entry tower on this house is visually chaotic and too narrow. The opening in the tower is too tall. The tower competes with the adjacent secondary mass and bay window. The brick archway conflicts with the triangular form above it, and the color contrasts of the stone and brick call attention to the flawed designed.

The secondary mass overwhelms entry element.

✓ Extend the main roofline down to the entry roofline.

The entry element is out of scale with the house.

✓ Lower and widen the opening; standardize the materials.

What **Not** to Build

The bay window competes with the front door.

✓ Create a two-story bay to unify the facade.

The shutter size is inappropriate for the windows.

✓ Remove the old shutters and replace with the correct size.

✓ What to **Build**

Simplifying and changing the scale

of the entry is the first step in correcting the design. Lowering the entry tower by continuing the downward slope of the roofline on the adjacent secondary mass and widening the base of the archway will accomplish this goal. Using brick and connecting the rooflines will frame the entry and give it the presence that was lacking originally. Correcting the shutter size and repeating the eyebrow arch above the garage doors are subtle changes that help create a more harmonious elevation.

DESIGN 101

Entry Feng Shui

Here are a few tips to help keep your front entry looking fresh.

- Keep the front walkway clean.

- Create symmetry with potted plants, shrubs, or other greenery that flank the front door.

- Groom all the plants and trees that lead to your front door.

- Ensure good lighting at sundown.

- Keep the glass in the front door and the sidelights clean.

- Clean and polish the hardware on the front door.

- Place flowers around the entrance to serve as a welcome to visitors.

- Use sheer material in sidelights—it will offer some privacy without blocking light.

DESIGN101

The Other Entry

Garage doors that face the street need extra attention. Integrating the garage doors into the overall design of the home is the best way to prevent them from overwhelming the exterior elevation. This can be accomplished in several ways:

- Repeat window patterns used on the house by adding transoms to the top of the garage doors.

- When using vinyl or steel doors, repeat the panels used in the front door, and paint the doors the same color as the rest of the trim on the home.

- Break up a three- or four-car garage door span with columns between the doors constructed of the same materials used on the house. Pilasters that match columns used near the entry or on porches can also be used.

- Place lanterns between the doors to create a sense of welcome.

- Add decorative hardware, such as handles or pulls, that match lanterns or door handles used on the rest of the home. These serve as accents and break up the monotony of large doors.

- Use wood trim painted a different color to break up the surface of the door and provide visual breaks.

- When using wood doors, repeat patterns found on other parts of the elevation or create a new pattern that is in keeping with the style of the home.

Creating patterns through the use of trim and decorative metal accents gives character and variety to this otherwise overwhelming garage span.

The linear pattern of the siding, the repeated window pattern, and the white trim all help to create an integrated entry.

This door is so well integrated that you are not even sure it is a garage. Repeating the color used on the porch and trim above anchors the facade.

This is an example of using window transoms within garage doors to break up the mass. The columns and the placement of the planters provide more detail and interest.

All of the materials used on this garage arrangement add to the architectural interest of the home. The wooden garage door is accented by the metal overhang and the series of clerestory windows.

Multiple Doors Lead Nowhere

This home has multiple doors on the front elevation. The only features distinguishing the entry from the other doors are the lanterns, but this is not enough to make the main door stand out from the others.

The front door blends in with other doors on the facade.

Add a larger, more distinctive door to differentiate it from the others.

What Not to Build

The entry lacks distinction.

Use landscaping to reinforce the importance of the entry.

The columns are too narrow for the structure.

Replace thin columns with more substantial columns.

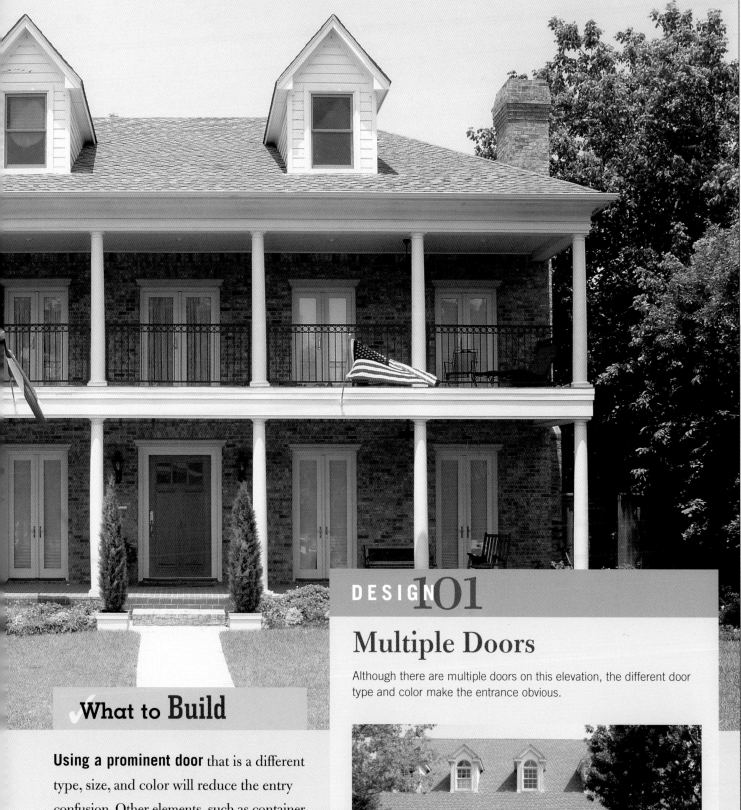

✓ What to Build

Using a prominent door that is a different type, size, and color will reduce the entry confusion. Other elements, such as container plantings, can add to the transition from yard to entrance.

DESIGN 101

Multiple Doors

Although there are multiple doors on this elevation, the different door type and color make the entrance obvious.

Overly Massive Doors

Large doors are often used to make a statement at an entry. Doors that are incorrectly scaled will stand out, but only because of their incompatibility with the rest of the elevation. These oversized doors are taller than the roof eave, which makes them appear more massive, upsetting the balance of the elevation.

The entry design appears inserted into the roof. The lack of wall plane beyond makes the arched entry incompatible with the rest of the facade.

Change the roof pitch to match the large gable. The wall plane creates a secondary mass proportional to adjacent main mass.

What Not to Build

The door is taller than roof eaves, creating an illusion of massive doors.

The new entry design allows the large door to match the scale of the entry element.

The scale of the doors is disproportionate to the entry feature.

One large door is better suited to a prominent entry.

✓ What to **Build**

One reason the original design was so unsettling was the lack of a wall plane behind the door. The entryway was simply inserted into the primary mass. The construction of a secondary mass utilizes a wall that provides a background, which changes the scale of the doors. Integration of the element with the use of similar materials and roof pitch creates an entranceway that is proportional to the entire facade.

DESIGN 101

Perfect Balance

The patterns in the sidelights and transom that surround the door create charm on this perfectly balanced facade. The surround is stately in its simplicity.

CHAPTER 3

Columns

Carrying the Weight

The column, or the post as it is often referred to in residential construction, has a long and rich history. There is evidence that columns were used 5,000 years ago in modest homes in the Middle East. Columns became design elements around 1500 BC in the temples and tombs of the Egyptian Pharaohs. A turning point in architecture occurred in Greece about 1,000 years later as Greek builders and masons found that metal dowels tied sections of columns together better than the standard grout joints that were common at the time.

To the ancient Greeks, proportions of the pieces that compose a column represented the perfect expression of beauty and harmony. All measurements were based on the diameter of the column, which determined the vertical dimension of the base, the capital, the overall height, and the spacing between columns. The orders of columns are: Doric, Ionic, Corinthian, Tuscan, and Composite. American residential design incorporates all of these types.

Columns are one of the primary structural elements used in homes. Made of wood, steel, concrete, masonry, or stone, columns can be purely ornamental or used to support compressive loads, such as the weight of floors, walls, and roofs. Technological advances allow for thinner, lighter, and stronger columns than those used in antiquity, yet the rules on how they should be used are as relevant today as they were thousands of years ago. Here is a guide to the sizing and placement of columns:

- Column Height – Single-story columns should be a minimum of 10 times the diameter or width of a column; a two-story column should be a minimum of 8 times the diameter or width.

- Column Spacing – Use an even number of columns to create an odd number of spaces.

- Beam, or entablature, depth – The beam depth should be 2 times the diameter or width of the columns supporting it.

- Beam, or entablature, thickness – The beam thickness should equal the diameter or width of the columns supporting it.

What to Build

Doubled slender columns create interest and a scale that is different from the scale created by one bulky column. This application expands the visual length of the porch and allows you to see through to the front wall of the home.

What to Build

Along with supporting the roof or porch at an entry, columns express a particular architectural style. These tapered columns on masonry bases are associated with the Arts and Crafts movement.

What to **Build**

Here's an example that uses columns of the Classical Order teamed with low-cost materials and a contemporary color scheme. The column height balances the roof mass. The even number of Tuscan columns creates an odd number of spaces. The depth of the entablature is double the diameter of the columns.

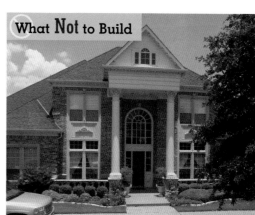

What **Not** to Build

The entablature is out of scale and overwhelms this entry. As the secondary mass of a home, projected entries should not compete with the larger primary mass of the elevation. The design should be a "house with an entablature" and not "an entablature with a house attached."

Too Tall for Comfort

Architectural elements often have a social connotation. Large columns are meant to be dramatic and present a sense of grandeur. Often times, architectural elements that intend to impress ignore fundamental architectural principles. On this home, the number of columns and their relationship to the facade behind them create a secondary mass that is not in proportion to the primary mass of the main part of the house. The two-story columns form an entry element that is too large and overwhelms the elevation.

The portico hides other architectural features.

Lower the portico to reveal well-designed dormers.

What Not to Build

The columns are out of scale.

The lower columns are in correct scale for the entablature above.

The entry feature is a secondary mass that is disproportionate to the primary mass behind it.

Lowering the columns brings the portico in scale with the rest of the house.

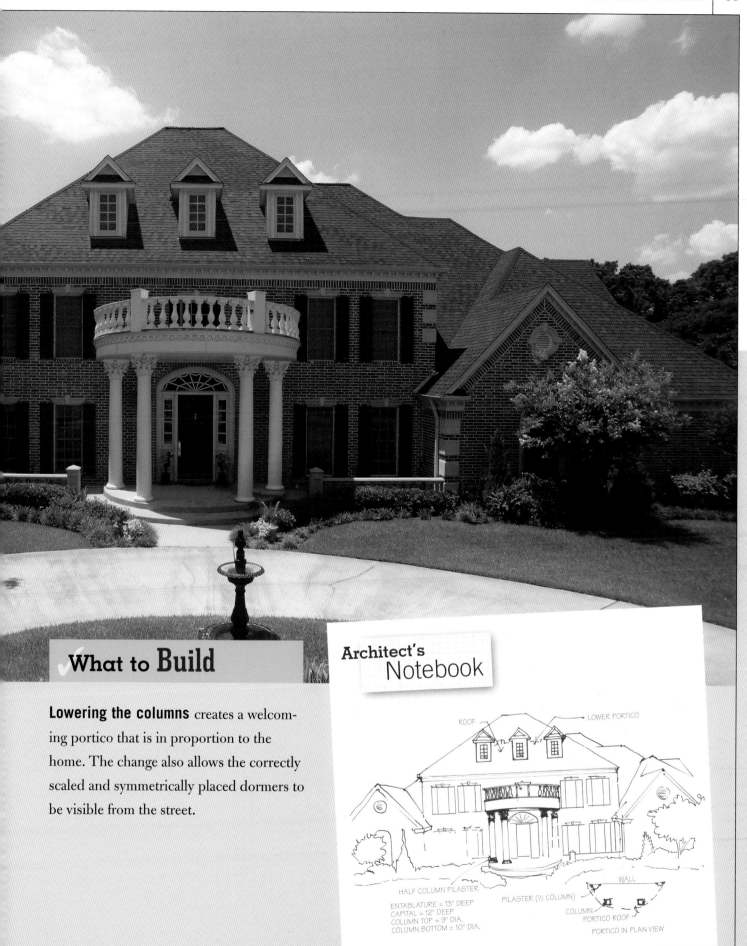

What to Build

Lowering the columns creates a welcoming portico that is in proportion to the home. The change also allows the correctly scaled and symmetrically placed dormers to be visible from the street.

Architect's Notebook

ROOF — LOWER PORTICO

HALF COLUMN PILASTER

ENTABLATURE = 13" DEEP
CAPITAL = 12" DEEP
COLUMN TOP = 9" DIA.
COLUMN BOTTOM = 10" DIA.

PILASTER (½ COLUMN)

WALL

COLUMN
PORTICO ROOF

PORTICO IN PLAN VIEW

Much Ado About Nothing

The main problem on this home is the relationship of the columns to the porch roof they support and, to a lesser degree, the type of column used. The scale of the very tall columns is out of proportion to the roof. If you were to increase the depth of the entablature, you would satisfy the rules of thumb, but you wouldn't solve the design dilemma. The ornate Corinthian capital is out of context with the other design elements on the elevation.

Corinthian capitals are unsuitable to the style of the home.

Use Doric capitals on columns to be consistent with the home's style.

The depth of entablature is disproportionate to the height of the column.

Add a pediment to correct the column height problem.

What Not to Build

The scale of the columns is disproportionate to the roof mass.

The new pediment corrects the proportion of the roof mass to the columns.

✓ What to Build

Adding a pediment to the porch roof balances the tall columns and creates a cohesive entry. Replacing the Corinthian capitals with Doric capitals fits with the style of the home. The combination of these corrections results in a well-balanced elevation.

DESIGN 101

Do the Math

To avoid monotony, vary the spacing between columns. The distances between the columns shown below are based on the 3-foot opening between the first two columns. The next opening is 3 times that, or 9 feet wide. The central opening is 1.5 times the original, or 4 feet 6 inches—followed by openings of 9 feet and, finally, 3 feet again. The closer spacing at each end anchors the porch, while the larger spacing allows the eye to carry past the column line to the symmetrically placed windows. The tighter central opening creates prominence that frames the front door.

Not Enough Support

At first glance, this case is an example of incorrectly proportioned column pairs that are too thin. A second look reveals the poorly executed relationship of the columns to the entry element. As constructed, the spindly columns support a facade that contains a semicircular opening, a detail that detracts from the rhythm created by the three gable ends. The additional roof overhang magnifies the problem by creating an "implied pediment," which projects past the facade. The white triangular returns at the bottom corners are out of place in this context.

White triangular returns are out of place.

The new entry does not include returns. Note the new window.

What Not to Build

The arch over the door breaks the rhythm created by the three gable ends.

Replace the arch with a pediment to create a cohesive entry element.

The columns are too narrow for what they are supporting.

Add wider columns to correct proportion.

✓ What to **Build**

Fixing individual problems will be unsuccessful unless the solutions are integrated into the overall composition. Here, the solution called for adding a beam, changing the column diameter, removing the triangular returns, and creating a pediment to form a cohesive entry element. Following the formula stated on page 48 and assuming a height of 84 inches, the column diameter should be a minimum of 8 inches; the beam, or entablature, should be two times the column diameter.

Architect's Notebook

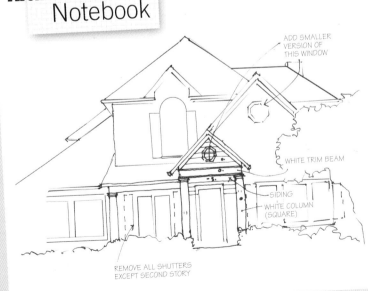

ADD SMALLER VERSION OF THIS WINDOW

WHITE TRIM BEAM

SIDING

WHITE COLUMN (SQUARE)

REMOVE ALL SHUTTERS EXCEPT SECOND STORY

Wrong Size, Wrong Style

There are several problems here. Functionally, the column diameter is large enough to support the weight of the roof; however, aesthetically the columns are too thin. The entablature is not deep enough and the corbels above the columns do not support the roof. The ornamental fretwork does not serve as a true capital. It also presents a stylistic dilemma: the French-Creole ironwork is not in keeping with this Federal-style home.

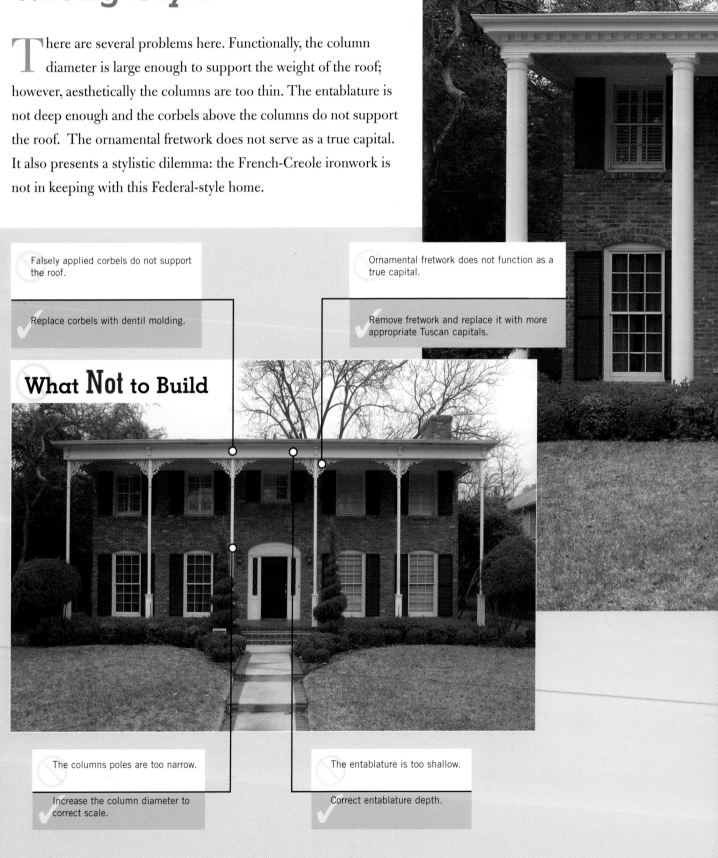

Falsely applied corbels do not support the roof.

✓ Replace corbels with dentil molding.

Ornamental fretwork does not function as a true capital.

✓ Remove fretwork and replace it with more appropriate Tuscan capitals.

What **Not** to Build

The columns poles are too narrow.

✓ Increase the column diameter to correct scale.

The entablature is too shallow.

✓ Correct entablature depth.

What to **Build**

Increasing the entablature depth and the column width create aesthetically pleasing proportions. The facade is improved by replacing the fretwork with a Tuscan capital, and the corbels with the dentil molding. All of these changes enhance the facade of the Federal-style home.

DESIGN 101

Don't Assume

People often assume that it is incorrect to place a column in front of a window. This faulty perception is based on the assumption that the viewer is always looking at the front elevation straight on from the center – a view often seen in photographs but rarely in real life. Homes are usually observed in motion as you walk or drive by. The column in front of the window dilemma is not a problem at all because the viewer, whether inside or outside of the house, can look to either side of the column. Other than placing a column in the middle of the path to the front door, placement should be dictated by the previously stated principles of number, spacing, scale, and proportion.

A Craftsman Mistake

A hallmark of the Arts and Crafts style is the short column shaft supported by a masonry base. The use of masonry to support the columns gives these homes an aura of substance. However in this case, the scale of the column shaft is out of proportion to the base. The brick base gets wider at the porch line, overwhelming the entire porch.

✓ What to Build

Correcting the column and brick base proportions draws the eye from the ground to the supporting beam. The column assembly is conveyed as a singular top to bottom visual element that is substantial but not overwhelming.

The height of the pier creates a massive element that dominates the front facade.

✓ Shorten the brick piers to accommodate longer columns.

What **Not** to Build

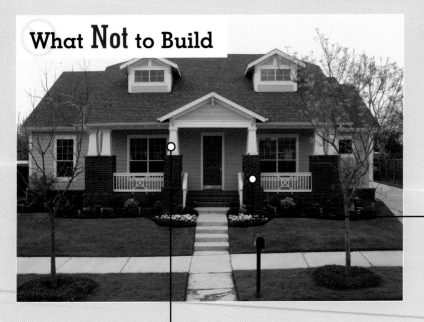

Truncated column shafts lead to incorrect proportions.

✓ Lengthening the column shafts creates correct proportions.

Even Numbers Only

Column spacing plays an important role in the appearance of an elevation. The odd number of columns disrupts the visual flow across the porch and partially obstructs the view of the front wall on the right side of the home.

✓ **What to Build**

Deleting the middle column on the right opens up the porch. Using an odd number of spaces between the columns is especially important because of the stout columns used here.

○ **What Not to Build**

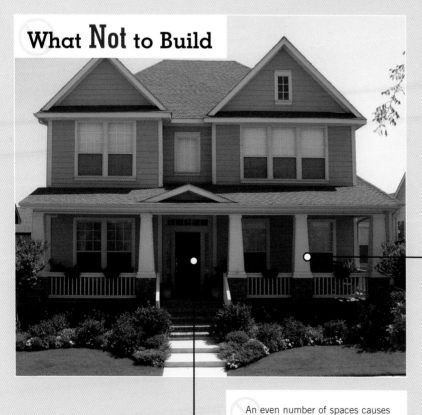

○ The middle column on the right is not necessary.

✓ Remove the middle column to achieve an even number.

○ An even number of spaces causes the eye to focus on the columns.

✓ Create an odd number of spaces by removing one column.

A Gathering Place

The front porch is an American icon. It speaks volumes about who we are as a nation—friendly, outgoing, and neighborly. Over the years, the porch has evolved and served a number of purposes, including shelter from the elements, additional sleeping space, and as a gathering place for friends and relatives.

Loggia, portico, piazza, and veranda all describe architectural spaces that have evolved into what we now call the porch. Historically, they were located to the side or rear of the house. But in America porches became a direct response to the climatic conditions of the New World—especially in the southern half of the country where heat and other environmental elements were a problem. Porches provided shade and helped keep the inside of the house cool. With the advent of air conditioning, the porch lost its pizzazz because it was no longer the coolest spot in the house.

Even if it has lost some of its functional uses, the porch is still an important feature in design today. When used correctly as a secondary mass or when integrated into the primary mass, it balances the facade of the home. The porch is an open living space that bridges the privacy of the home with the public community of the neighborhood. Keys to good porch design include:

- Porches should not dominate the facade. The length and width of the porch should be in proportion to the rest of the house.

- The porch material should match or flow with the rest of the elevation.

- Use columns correctly. There should be an even number of columns producing an odd number of spaces between the columns.

- The porch should be deep enough to accommodate furniture.

- The entablature ratio must be correct—the entablature (beam) depth should be two times column diameter.

- When adding a porch to an existing building, let the existing architecture dictate the style of the porch.

✓ What to **Build**

This full-width porch is well integrated into the overall design. The paired columns and pediment help define the entry.

What to **Build**

A deep arcaded porch shades and cools the interior living space.

A side porch creates an outdoor living space. Historically, a side porch served as a sleeping area during warmer weather.

The front porch creates a transition between the privacy of our homes and the rest of the community.

Porch versus Entry

The oversized entry gable is out of scale and disproportionate to the rest of the elevation. This dominant element—with its oversized vent—distorts the perception of the front door, making it appear too small. The varying column widths and the erratic spacing call attention to the columns instead of the porch.

The entry gable is too large and disproportionate to the mass behind it.

Delete the oversized gable to balance the elevation.

The shed dormer looks out of place.

Replace the shed dormer with a gable dormer to balance the second story.

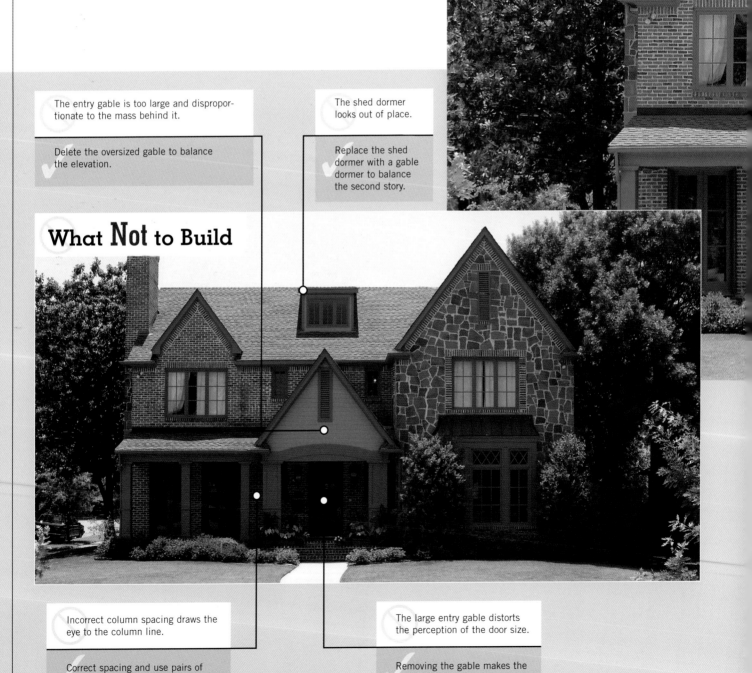

What **Not** to Build

Incorrect column spacing draws the eye to the column line.

Correct spacing and use pairs of columns to establish entry hierarchy.

The large entry gable distorts the perception of the door size.

Removing the gable makes the door a more visible focal point.

✓ **What to Build**

Deleting the gable end and creating a continuous porch roofline directs the focus to the porch instead of to the massive structure above. Changing the brick on the chimney to stone helps offset the heavy gable end on the right. Replacing the shed dormer with a wall dormer brings uniformity to the roofline. The column pairs, in tandem with the wall dormer centered over the doorway, create an integrated porch with a pleasant entry.

Architect's Notebook

USE WOOD TRIM

DELETE SHED DORMER   BRICK

REPLACE BRICK WITH STONE

LIKE WINDOW BELOW

MOVE

BRICK ROOFING

REMOVE

EQUAL SPACE   EQUAL SPACE   USE THIS COLUMN TO CREATE THESE FOUR

The Truncated Porch

The heavy entablature—the section supported by the columns—creates a strong visual focus that detracts from this brick home. It is double the recommended size, making the columns, windows, and door seem smaller than they really are. An entablature should have a 2:1 ratio. The entablature depth should be two times the column diameter.

The entablature to column ratio is 4:1 and compresses the columns.

Correct entablature depth allows the top of the doors and window to be visible.

What to **Build**

Decreasing the visual weight of the entablature and raising the columns balances the elevation. The portico is proportionate to the primary mass behind it, allowing the transom above the door and the top of the windows to become visible from the street. The white wooden rockers provide a relaxing place to sit on this welcoming porch.

What **Not** to Build

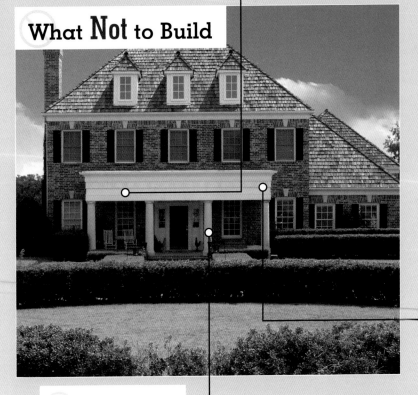

The mass of entablature is out of proportion to the front facade.

Make the size of the entablature proportionate to the front facade.

The column height is too short for the portico.

New entablature allows for the correct column height.

A Distracting View

The simple palette of green siding and white trim used on this house is abandoned at the porch with the introduction of stone and an unfinished wood railing. Although the correct number of columns is used, their erratic placement is visually disturbing.

An inconsistent eave line disrupts integration of the porch roof.

✓ Create a continuous eave to integrate expansive roof.

What to **Build**

Removing the stonework and painting the columns and railing white visually integrates the porch with the rest of the materials on the house. A uniform placement of columns creates a sequential rhythm and helps to frame the entry.

What **Not** to Build

Erratic placement of columns creates disorder.

✓ Change column spacing to establish a pleasing rhythm.

The introduction of different materials detracts from the design.

✓ Match materials to incorporate the porch elements into the design.

Pocket-Sized Porch

The covered patio is forced into the center of this home and conflicts with the arched opening at the entrance. This area is too shallow to be functional and serves no purpose. By removing the porch and widening the entry, the porch/entry conflict is resolved. Raising the window in the center creates a balance with the window on the left.

✓ **What to Build**

The porch is forced into the facade, detracting from the entry and causing visual confusion.

✓ Remove the entire porch to balance the facade.

What Not to Build

The patio is too shallow to be used.

✓ Open area allows more room for the patio.

DESIGN 101

The Faux Porch

The word porch evokes images for everyone—whether it's an old blue Victorian with a wraparound veranda filled with white wicker furniture or a tiny lakeside bungalow with a worn rocker in the corner of a well-used retreat. Porches are people-friendly, an open inviting space to relax and escape to. The versatility of these outdoor living areas, both architecturally and stylistically, is what makes them unique. They can be in front, in back, on the side, or wrapped around the top or bottom of a home. They may reflect the style of the architecture, be painted a bolder hue, or decorated to follow the changing seasons.

Porches trigger strong feelings in people, but in an attempt to use porches to make their houses more appealing, some builders fall short of incorporating the true spirit of community in the porch design. The new porches are too shallow and serve no practical use. Like a stage set, many modern porches are used as props to elicit an emotional response from us. Using elaborate spindlework for the rails or applying a decorative frieze suspended from the porch ceiling carries on the charade. These tacked on faux porches create an illusion but aren't deep enough to be used as true living spaces.

This poorly integrated faux porch is pushed under the roofline and is too shallow, serving only as an overhang with columns. The contrasting colors magnify the incorrect ratio of the oversized entablature and narrow columns.

What Not to Build

What to Build

This well-integrated porch has the correct column-to-entablature ratio and is deep enough for furnishings. The yellow siding and classic white trim flow seamlessly across the elevation.

Imbalanced Facade

The center element is the primary focus of this home and over-whelms the entrance. The asymmetrical porch with multiple arches and the different window styles create an imbalanced and cluttered elevation.

Create a new gable feature to establish entry focal point.

What **Not** to Build

An asymmetrical porch creates imbalance in the facade.

Extend the porch so that the entry is in the center.

The two-story element is the focal point, detracting from the entry.

An extended porch reduces importance of the two-story element.

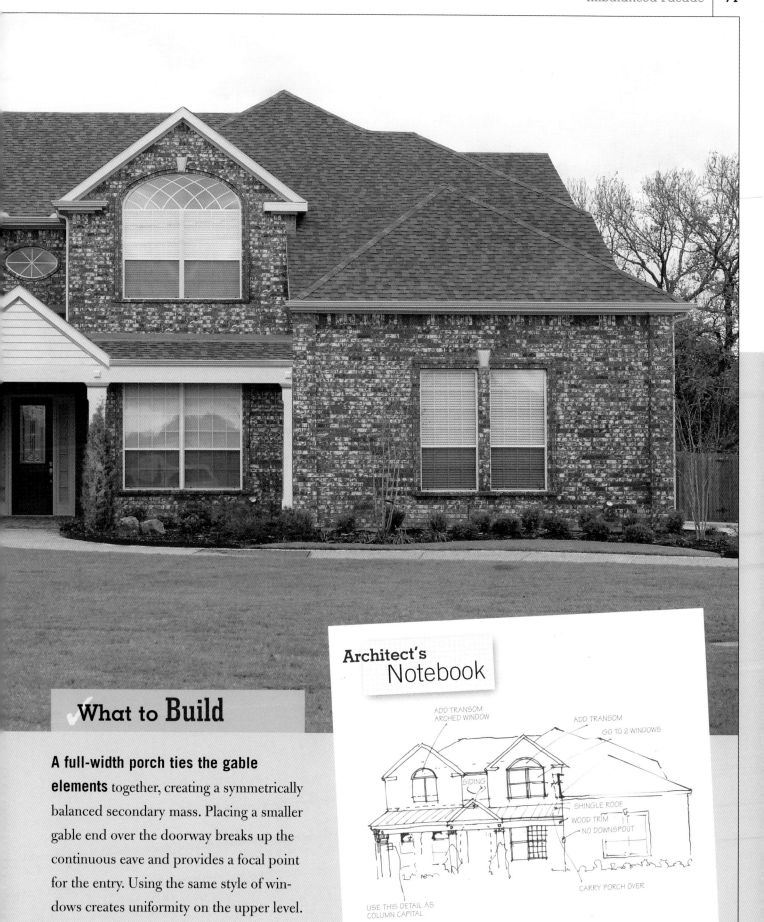

✓ What to **Build**

A full-width porch ties the gable elements together, creating a symmetrically balanced secondary mass. Placing a smaller gable end over the doorway breaks up the continuous eave and provides a focal point for the entry. Using the same style of windows creates uniformity on the upper level.

Architect's Notebook

ADD TRANSOM ARCHED WINDOW

ADD TRANSOM
GO TO 2 WINDOWS

SIDING

SHINGLE ROOF
WOOD TRIM
NO DOWNSPOUT

CARRY PORCH OVER

USE THIS DETAIL AS COLUMN CAPITAL

DESIGN 101

Perfect Porches

Porches that are well integrated into the design of the home add character as well as additional living space. The use of a porch provides an element of depth and balance to a flat facade. As shown in the following examples, detailing can be ornate or conservative and should complement the design of the home.

Victorian Flavor

This is a classic example of a wraparound porch that is well proportioned and integrated into the home's overall design. The front porch cocoons the home and divides the public walkway from the private residence. Visual flow is established with the consistent use of trim and siding throughout the elevation.

- This shallow roof pitch creates a horizontal line that divides the first and second story.
- The white trim is consistent with the other detailing.
- The expansive porch is integrated into the overall design.

Good Thing in a Small Package

This well-integrated and functional porch creates a secondary mass that balances the gable end and the primary mass beyond. The use of white rails and perfectly scaled columns blends the porch with the rest of the home. There is enough depth to allow the outdoor living space to be functional.

- Although small, the porch is deep enough to be useful.
- The columns and railing suit the porch and house.

Historical Accuracy

Integrating historical aspects into the design of your home adds character that is usually only found in older homes. The shorter columns reflect the height of the second story and are in proportion to the overall elevation. Varying the column capitals is a subtle change that gives interest to the balcony.

- This second-story balcony is integrated into the entire porch element, which divides the two-story height into a human scale.

- Balconies, such as the one shown here, historically would have been screened-in and used as sleeping areas.

A Welcoming Sight

The correct proportions elicit a comfortable feel to the formal details of this eclectic design. The roofline flows seamlessly into the adjoining portions of the home, and the materials complement one another. When creating a porch that is nestled within the rest of the elevation, the correct scale, balance, and materials are especially important.

- The pitch of the porch roof flows into the main roof.

- The correct scale of the porch components creates a horizontal line that terminates into the focal point of the gable-end projection.

A Perfect Fit

This full-width porch utilizes the correct scale—which includes the column height and width and the entablature ratio—to form a stately expression on a modest home. Placing a few pieces of furniture on the porch creates a welcoming attitude toward your neighbors.

- A simple design does not overwhelm the facade.

- Furniture, plants, and accessories add subtle welcoming touches.

CHAPTER **5**

Windows

Shaping Light

Windows, originally called "wind-holes," evolved from actual holes in the wall to design elements that dictate the style and mood of a home. In the past, oiled cloths, translucent papers, fabrics, or skins covered window openings. Window glass was first introduced in Europe in the seventeenth century and was costly to produce.

Windows are a key piece of the design puzzle. When windows are placed solely for interior consideration, the design of the exterior suffers. Integrating the windows to allow the interior space adequate light and views, while also keeping the exterior elevation in balance, is important.

The scale, style, and rhythm of windows determine the personality of a home. Creating patterns with windows or using windows as accents adds interest to an elevation. The number and placement of windows dictate how you achieve proportions and rhythm.

The window choices today are staggering, so it is important to understand which windows work best with your elevation. Key elements of window design include the following:

- Use no more than two shapes to avoid visual clutter.

- Using the same window type and trim across the elevation will help maintain visual order.

- Vertically align windows that are located one above the other.

- Windows on the second story should be smaller or equal in size to the ground-level windows.

- Line up window heads horizontally on each level.

- To create a horizontal emphasis, use a band of windows.

- Small windows in gables create visual interest.

- Muntin patterns, the molding between windows, should be consistent. Decorative accent windows are an exception.

What to Build

The series of copper-clad wooden windows are a perfect design choice for creating personal style and interest on an elevation.

What Not to Build

The different shape, style, and trim of the adjacent windows lack visual unity. Using the same materials and style creates uniformity across an elevation.

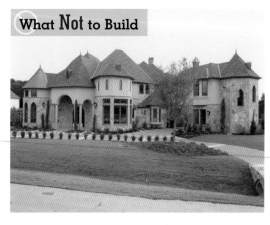

What Not to Build

There are seven different window shapes in this elevation. When viewed in combination with the varied roof forms and odd application of materials, the visual clutter creates a disoriented design.

✓ **What to Build**

Stained-glass windows add character and can be used as accents or focal points on an elevation. They also provide privacy by obscuring a view while still allowing light to enter.

Correcting an Overpowering Presence

The expansive bay window with both upper and lower cornice is disproportionate to the secondary mass and dwarfs the entrance.

The two-story bay window dominates the facade.

Add a series of smaller windows to break up the stone mass.

What **Not** to Build

The wooden arch is misused at the entry, creating an imbalance.

Adding a stone column on the left frames and focuses the entry.

The light to the right of the entry is misplaced.

Centering the light above the entry provides visual height.

✓ What to **Build**

Removing the window assembly

altogether and replacing it with two smaller windows would only be a partial solution. Break up the large stone mass by adding a series of correctly scaled windows to take the place of the large window assembly. Relocating the light above the lintel provides visual height to the entry. Removing the wood and filling in the left side of the entry with stone provides the proper scale.

Architect's Notebook

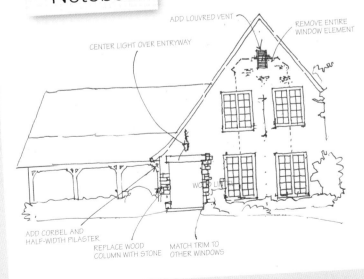

ADD LOUVRED VENT

REMOVE ENTIRE WINDOW ELEMENT

CENTER LIGHT OVER ENTRYWAY

WOOD LINT

ADD CORBEL AND HALF-WIDTH PILASTER

REPLACE WOOD COLUMN WITH STONE

MATCH TRIM TO OTHER WINDOWS

A Bottom–Heavy Design

The bright white trim on the first-floor windows cuts off the arched transoms and shortens the perceived window height, emphasizing the incorrect window proportions on this two-story home.

The round clerestory is out of proportion to the brick mass.

✔ Elongate this window to correct vertical scale and repeat the form of the door.

Some second-floor windows look taller than the first-floor units.

✔ Lower the head height to make second-story windows slightly shorter than those on the first floor.

What Not to Build

White trim shortens the perceived height of the window.

✔ Remove detailing, and change the trim color to correct the vertical scale for the first-floor windows.

The use of different trim detail is visually disturbing.

✔ Use the same trim detail and color to create visual order.

DESIGN 101

Window Pediments

These window pediments are separated from the window assemblies by a beltline. When used as a window accent, a pediment should always be part of the window assembly. Integrating the pediments with the windows creates taller windows that reflect the proportions of the interior rooms on the exterior facade.

✓ What to Build

To correct the window scale, remove the trim detail to expose the transoms. Lowering the head height of the second-floor windows by 1 foot corrects the scale of these windows as they relate to those on the ground level. Elongating the clerestory window for correct proportion and differentiating it in scale from the round louvers at the other gables enhance the entry. Treat clerestory windows at an entry as an accent, but they should share common features with other windows on the elevation.

Bay Watch

Bay windows are used to extend a room and create a visual focal point. The projecting bay windows on this home are forced into the space on either side of the entrance and are out of scale.

The pair of bay windows competes with the front door as the focal point.

✓ Correctly scaled windows create symmetrical balance at the entry.

What **Not** to Build

False ornamentation shutters cannot cover the window when closed.

✓ Remove shutters, as they are not appropriate for new bay windows.

These bay windows are out of scale in relation to the wall space.

✓ Switch bay windows with double-hung units on the ends of the house.

✔ What to Build

By reversing the location of the bay and the double-hung windows on the facade and adjusting their size, all of the windows now serve their correct purpose. The windows flanking the entrance are symmetrically balanced and are correctly scaled. The addition of a clerestory window creates a strong visual focus at the gable entry.

Architect's Notebook

ADD A CLERESTORY WINDOW

CORRECTLY SCALED WINDOWS CREATE SYMMETRICAL BALANCE

DOUBLE-HUNG WINDOWS HERE

REMOVE SHUTTERS

BAY WINDOWS HERE
BASICALLY, REVERSE WINDOW TYPES

DESIGN 101

Good Window Treatments

Using Clerestory Windows

Clerestory refers to the upper portion of a wall that contains windows located above the normal window height. The clerestory windows above this garage door admit light while maintaining privacy and security. The straightforward rhythm established by the five equally spaced windows adds interest to what would otherwise be a blank wall.

- The height of the windows admits natural light while maintaining privacy.

- The number and placement of the windows provide a design rhythm.

- The clerestory windows provide interest and balance the visual dominance of the garage door.

Distinctive Trimwork

Using taller windows on the lower level of a two-story home establishes prominence on the ground plane. This follows the ceiling height proportions for both interior floors and creates balance on the outside elevation. The decorative wood trim around the windows follows the same pattern of the surround at the entry and gives visual uniformity to the ground level.

- The use of different scale windows, taller on the first floor and shorter on the second, balances the exterior facade.

- Smaller windows on the second floor provide correct proportion to shorter second-floor ceiling height.

- Taller windows are proportionate to inner room volume on the lower level.

In Good Order

The vertical and horizontal alignment of the windows creates visual order. Using an ascending window height ratio of 3:2:1 creates the correct proportions in the gable end. The window patterns are reinforced at the entrance transom and sidelights.

- An ascending 3:2:1 window ratio creates correct proportion at the gable-end secondary mass.

- Vertical alignment creates visual order.

- Rectangular panes continue the theme of the design.

The Traditional Approach

Aesthetic perception is strongly influenced by a sense of order. Repeating patterns of windows, such as those around the door, give continuity to your design. When deciding overall window placement, remember that aligning windows is your primary tool in creating visual order.

- Symmetrical window placement in the upper level creates a strong visual flow.

- Vertical placement of windows creates visual order.

- The transom repeats the pattern of the sidelights for visual continuity.

- Window sidelights reinforce the elevation symmetry.

Textbook Design

Although there are too many columns, the descending scale of the window elements reinforces the hierarchy of the interior spaces and creates a proportional balance as the secondary mass narrows toward the top.

- A clerestory window creates visual interest at the gable.

- The windows become progressively smaller.

- Vertical alignment creates a visual order in the secondary mass.

In Need of a Realignment

This home was designed with a focus on how the windows looked from the interior of the house; the exterior facade was an afterthought. The imbalanced elevation is further exaggerated through the use of a different window type and a change in trim color.

The windows are not vertically aligned.

Align the windows to bring order to the facade.

What **Not** to Build

The window hood mold is out of scale and does not flow with the elevation.

Remove the hood mold to standardize trim around the windows.

The second-floor windows do not align horizontally.

Create a pleasing horizontal arrangement by aligning the window tops.

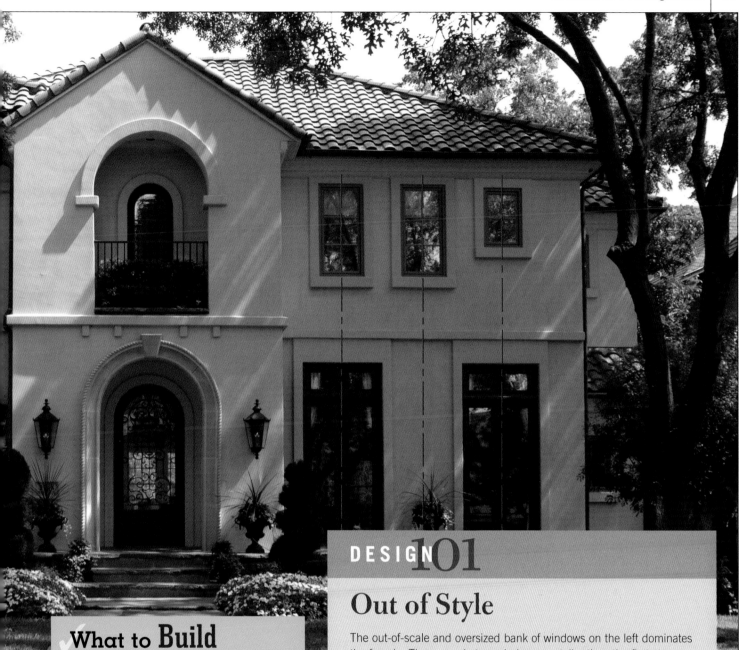

DESIGN 101

Out of Style

The out-of-scale and oversized bank of windows on the left dominates the facade. The second-story windows are taller than the first-story windows, distorting the perceived interior ceiling height from the outside. Large walls of glass are common in contemporary style homes as focal points. When placed on a traditional style, the scale and proportion can be incorrect and out of place stylistically.

✓ ## What to **Build**

Although the floor plan may dictate where these windows are placed, the exterior elevation can be partially corrected by eliminating the odd window type, using vertical alignment where possible—see the red dashes above—and using a consistent trim color. An ornamental tree planted on the left will cover the blank wall and balance the elevation with the windows on the right.

Disparate Window Types

Several mullion patterns and multiple window shapes, including round arch, rectangular, and basket-handle arch, create visual clutter. The solution is to simplify window shapes and delete the multiple windowpane patterns. Downsizing the windows will also create the correct proportions where needed.

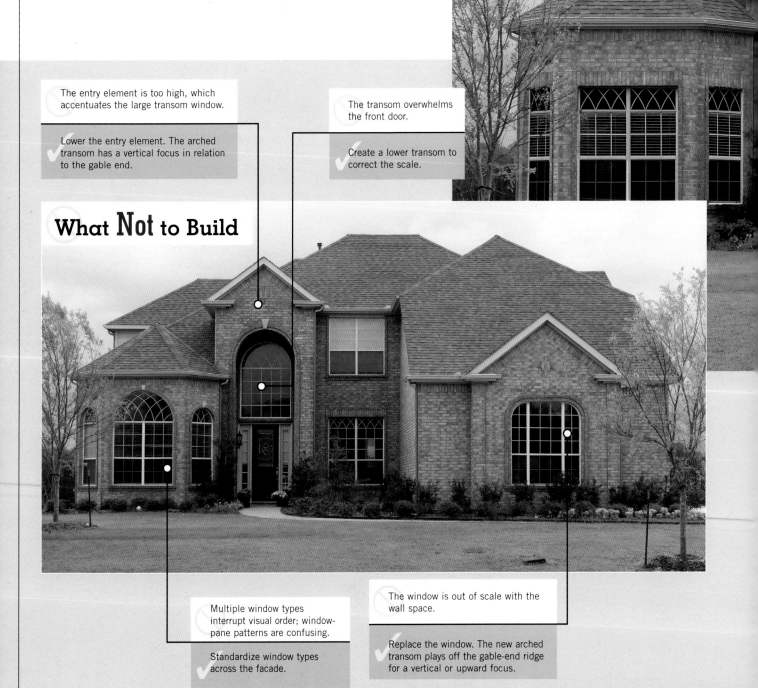

The entry element is too high, which accentuates the large transom window.

Lower the entry element. The arched transom has a vertical focus in relation to the gable end.

The transom overwhelms the front door.

Create a lower transom to correct the scale.

What Not to Build

Multiple window types interrupt visual order; window-pane patterns are confusing.

Standardize window types across the facade.

The window is out of scale with the wall space.

Replace the window. The new arched transom plays off the gable-end ridge for a vertical or upward focus.

✓ What to **Build**

Simplifying the muntin patterns across the elevation and changing the shapes of the windows unifies the facade. Design logic calls for using the rounded arch at the gable ends. Lowering the roofline and window above the entry corrects the scale and proportion of the front entrance.

Architect's Notebook

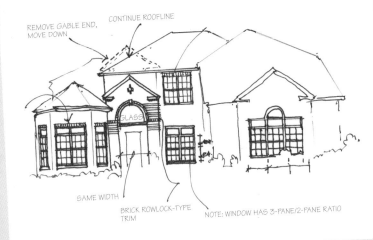

REMOVE GABLE END, MOVE DOWN

CONTINUE ROOFLINE

GLASS

SAME WIDTH

BRICK ROWLOCK-TYPE TRIM

NOTE: WINDOW HAS 3-PANE/2-PANE RATIO

Cut the Clutter

The exuberant quality of this residence is part of its charm. However, too many windows, multiple shutters, questionable placement, and the introduction of different patterns is distracting. Adding to the clutter is the variation in window headers, which includes arched brick on the right, straight rowlock on the lower left, white lintel on the top left, and a white arch on the clerestory above the front entry.

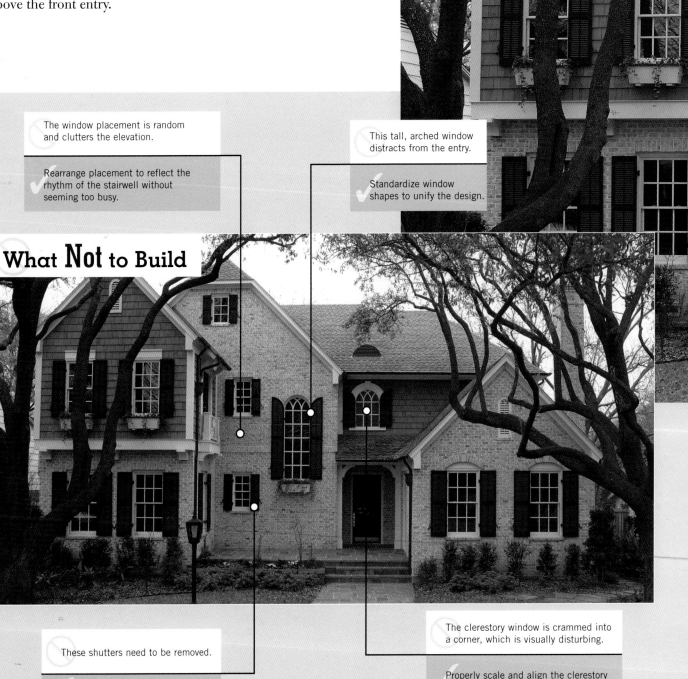

The window placement is random and clutters the elevation.

Rearrange placement to reflect the rhythm of the stairwell without seeming too busy.

This tall, arched window distracts from the entry.

Standardize window shapes to unify the design.

What **Not** to Build

These shutters need to be removed.

Remove shutters on the primary mass.

The clerestory window is crammed into a corner, which is visually disturbing.

Properly scale and align the clerestory window with the front door.

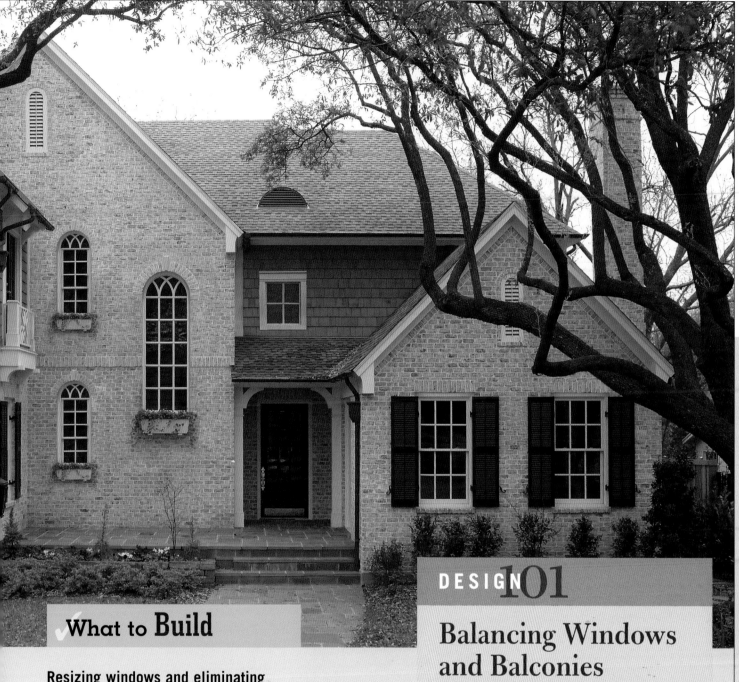

✓ What to Build

Resizing windows and eliminating some shutters unifies and balances the facade. The center windows reflect the pattern of the interior stairwell, and the window headers on the lower level are uniform across the elevation.

DESIGN 101

Balancing Windows and Balconies

This balcony assembly, below right, is in correct proportion to the window below: The added shutters on the first story give visual weight and increase the perceived window width.

CHAPTER **6**

Selecting Materials

The Art of Application

Builders and homeowners select the materials they use on their homes based on appearance, style, and durability. But in an attempt to make homes distinctive and individualized, homeowners often add more materials, patterns, and textures than are necessary, resulting in visual chaos. If you are building a new home or addition, research the materials you plan on using before construction begins.

The human body has often been used as a model for natural beauty. Its parts compare to the parts of a house. The walls are equivalent to the skin. The windows are the eyes of the facade. Just as the eyes on a face should resemble each other, so should the windows on a house. The roof of a home is comparable to a head of hair and can either complement the exterior design or detract from it. Adding elements of ornamentation is like putting on jewelry—often, less is more.

The goal is to avoid adding too many materials to the elevation. Each house must have a roof, walls, and windows. These elements all require separate types of materials. Adding more materials changes the relationship among them. To help in that regard, we developed the "Rule of Five." It is a point system that helps you avoid adding too many materials to the outside of your house. (For more information, see page 98.) Tips for materials selection includes:

- To help a small house look wider, use a horizontal material, such as clapboard siding.

- When using two materials in a wall plane, place the visually heavier material on the bottom.

- Contrasting textures can be used together.

- When mixing materials, use the more ornate materials to provide emphasis.

- Use a contrasting color or texture to highlight specific parts of the elevation.

What to Build

The contrast between the textures of the rough clay roof, the smooth stucco walls, and the rustic shutters allows you to appreciate each element.

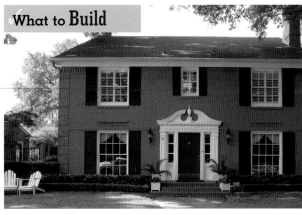

What to Build

The contrasting colors give definition to the elements on this home. The white surround, red door, and black shutters create a complementary pallet.

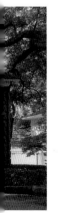

What **Not** to Build

The use of different materials gives this home a splitting, or "duplex", effect. It looks smaller than it actually is because the eyes move from side to side rather than seeing the house as a whole. If you divide this house in half, it looks like two houses rather than one.

What to **Build**

The use of stone draws attention to the entry and clearly differentiates it from the rest of the elevation.

Making a Few Changes

Changing a few aspects of this home will improve the elevation. From a materials aspect, this home should be all siding. Arched windows are rarely seen on this style of home and need to be changed. The pediment, which is not integrated into the porch roofline, competes with the bay window structure on the left.

These windows should not be arched.

Rectangular windows are historically accurate and have the correct proportions.

What Not to Build

Brick does not belong here.

Replace brick with siding that matches the rest of the house.

The raised entry feature interrupts the eave line of the porch, causing an imbalance in the elevation.

Revise the entry to create a continuous eave. This will balance the right side of this elevation.

✓ What to Build

This sub-type of Victorian architecture
typically has a dominant gable at the front,
an asymmetrical facade with a porch, and
uses ornamentation to avoid a monotonous
elevation. Redesigning the entry pediment
so that it is part of the porch roof creates a
sense of balance. While brick is appropriate
on the chimney, its use on the left side of
the house is out of place. Changing the
brick to siding will give a better sense of
material continuity.

DESIGN 101

The Wrong Element

Solid stone is too heavy to be suspended from
stucco as it is shown here. The strength and
solidarity of stone is negated when it is placed
as an appliqué or veneer that is not possible to
construct. When using stone, it should appear as
a supporting, not suspended, element.

DESIGN 101

The Rule of Five

This point system allows you to tally materials and avoid "over-materializing" the exterior elevation. The three main elements of the home—roof, walls, and windows—automatically receive one point each. Each additional material receives a point. The key is to never go over 5, and in many cases a score of 3 or 4 is best.

Example:

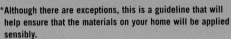

Element	Material	Point
Roof	Clay	+ 1
Walls	Stucco	+ 1
Windows	Rectangular	+ 1
	SUBTOTAL	3
Additional materials		
Walls	Stone	+ 1
Windows	Palladian	+ 1
	GRAND TOTAL	5

*Although there are exceptions, this is a guideline that will help ensure that the materials on your home will be applied sensibly.

ELEMENT	MATERIAL	POINT
Roof	Asphalt shingles	+ 1
Walls	Siding	+ 1
Windows	Rectangular	+ 1
	SUBTOTAL	3
ADDITIONAL MATERIALS		0
	GRAND TOTAL	3

ELEMENT	MATERIAL	POINT
Roof	Asphalt shingles	+ 1
Walls	Brick	+ 1
Windows	Rectangular	+ 1
	SUBTOTAL	3
ADDITIONAL MATERIALS		
Roof	Metal	+1
Walls	Stone and stucco	+2
Windows	Eyebrow	+1
	GRAND TOTAL	7

Clashing Colors

The brick on the first level and the shingles that cover the gable on this home shown below are viewed as separate elements and not part of an integrated design. On smaller houses, busy looking materials tend to visually shrink the primary mass. This makes the house appear smaller than it really is.

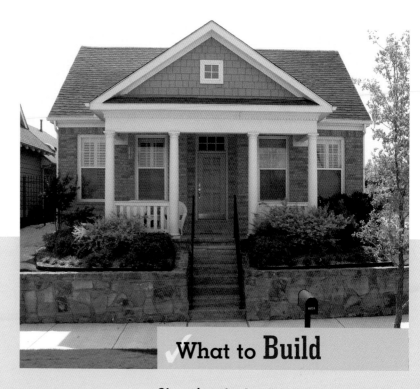

What to **Build**

Changing the house to one material would solve the problem. Another solution is to use brick and siding colors that are consistent with one another. This strategy will keep the view focused on the home as a whole.

What **Not** to Build

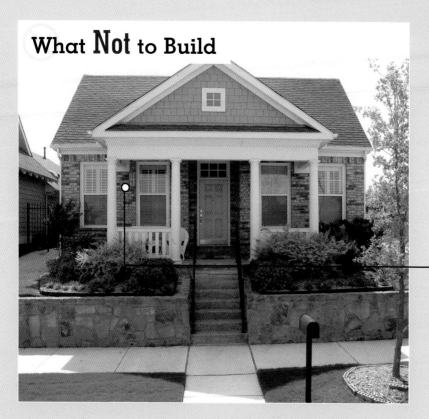

Two different materials make the house appear small.

Change the color of the brick to make it consistent with the siding.

Brick Breaks the Flow

The brick secondary mass on the left of the house shown below is visually heavier than the siding, skewing the focus of the elevation. The house appears lopsided.

✓ **What to Build**

Changing the brick to siding extends the horizontal lines of the house. This makes the house appear wider and balances the overall elevation.

The secondary mass is too heavy due to the use of brick.

✓ Continue the siding to the secondary mass. This widens the house and balances the elevation.

What Not to Build

DESIGN 101

The Rules for Patterns

Pattern Rule #1

Repeating a pattern consisting of different materials creates rhythm on a facade.

Repeating patterns create a particular theme or story for the home. In the Art Deco period, a lily motif represented happiness. In the Colonial South, pineapples symbolized wealth. The bow-tie ribbon design was a favorite of builders of Victorian houses. In the photo above, the design is found in the ornamental detailing and the stained glass windows, not shown.

Pattern Rule #2

The directional aspect of a material can affect proportion, perception of scale, and massing. It is best to only use one or two patterns; more can create unsettling visual breaks.

This house uses brick in two different patterns. The brick changes direction only once at the gable ends, which follows Rule #2.

Pattern Rule #3

When mixing two materials, apply each material in a consistent direction.

Although brick and stone are mixed on this house, the stone runs horizontally and the brick runs vertically. This is consistent with Rule #3. Diagonally placed materials are considered to be vertical when placed at the gable ends.

Rule Breaker

This house uses brick in three different patterns. The brick is first applied in a horizontal pattern, then a herringbone pattern, and changes direction again at the eaves. The pattern changes within the same vertical plane, creating visual breaks.

Material Overload

The mixture of materials on this home breaks The Rule of Five and The Rules for Patterns. (See pages 98 and 101.) This house receives a materials score of six. The brick runs horizontally over part of the house and in a basket-weave pattern on the upper portion of the elevation. There is also a very chaotic roofline.

Two brick patterns are used on the same elevation.

Give all brick a horizontal orientation.

Stone and brick divide the secondary mass.

Use stone on the entire secondary mass.

What Not to Build

Dormers disrupt the roofline.

Remove the dormers to make the roofline consistent.

This window shape is not consistent with the others.

Make all windows rectangular.

DESIGN 101

Unnatural Use of Materials

Many of the masonry materials shown here are used inappropriately. Stone is a strong material, yet here it is used on Tudor-style patterns that are usually formed using wood. Brick is used inappropriately in the window heads and mullions where wood would be a better choice. The lentil and keystone above the balcony is not really a structural component as it should be, but appears tacked on because you can see brick above, below, and behind it. The double X pattern on the left side clashes with the other patterns.

✓ What to Build

By making the relatively simple change of making all of the windows rectangular, this house's score drops to five, but the facade will remain visually confusing. By separating the materials and confining the use of stone to the secondary masses—in this case the circular portion of the elevation, the chimney, gable-end projections, and in a narrow band under the beltline—the elevation looks better organized. The horizontal orientation of the brick establishes continuity of design, as does eliminating the dormers to establish a consistent roofline.

DESIGN 101

Material Matters

Built to Last

This home uses an interesting combination of two masonry products in the same wall plane. The monotone colors create a large mass with subtle secondary mass divisions. The brick beltline separates the floor levels. The weighty rusticated texture of the stone on the base level supports the lighter tan brick that forms the second story. The red tile roof relates to the brick trim color and caps the home with another material that represents permanence.

- Brick forms the second-level band.
- The beltline divides the home into levels.
- Rusticated stone acts as the base level.
- Clay tile caps the home with another durable material.

The Exception to the Rule

There are times when the style of a home dictates the use of more materials than usual and The Rule of Five can be broken. This home combines multiple effective techniques in applying materials. Stucco consistently defines the second floor. Decorative half-timbering reinforces the rhythm of the gable ends. A change in brick pattern and a stone surround at the archway emphasize the hierarchy of the entry element.

- Half-timbers reinforce the rhythm of the gable ends.
- The change in the brick pattern and the stone surround emphasize the entry hierarchy.
- This design uses stucco only on the second floor.

Elegant Simplicity

The use of stone creates a stout or formidable presence within the design. The contrast in materials between the roof and wall highlights the rusticated texture of the stone and smooth nature of the metal. The complementary colors combine with a minimal palette to compose a straightforward elegance.

- The smoothness of the metal creates a simple roof plane.
- Tan and gray create a complementary color palate.
- Sophisticated stone has a formidable presence.

Soothing Stucco

Stucco is the unifying element on this house, creating primary mass, wall planes, ornamental detailing in the form of quoins, and trim. A complementary scheme of muted colors portrays a refined design sense. The use of annual and perennial flowers in the foreground provides accent color and animation.

- The wall planes, trim, and ornamental details are made of stucco.
- The complementary color scheme unifies the design.
- Flowers work as accents that provide color in the foreground.

Pretty in Pink

The use of a minimal number of materials reinforces the simplicity of this design. Although the roof and walls are in the same color scheme, the contrast between the rough and smooth textures of the materials gives this home its unique appearance. Stucco is flexible in its ability to display large areas of color. The color used on this home transforms this simple idea to a bold expression. Even the landscaping follows the color scheme.

- Pastel colors have a Caribbean connotation.
- The simple color scheme (pink and gray) is consistent in its application.
- The color of the flowers accents the color scheme.

DESIGN 101

Watching Your Weight

When mixing materials, it is important that they are placed in the proper positions. As a rule, position heavy materials on the bottom of a wall and light materials on top. The heavier material should appear to be supporting the lighter material. Although many materials are available in lightweight veneers, keep the natural weight of the intended material in mind. Viewers do not see elements as veneers, but rather interpret them for what they represent. For example, stucco can support a stone veneer, but could never support real stone.

What **Not** to Build

Stone is a heavy and bulky material. In this example, stone is used above stucco, making the house appear top-heavy. When stone is used on the second level, it must have stone below it as a visual support. Either bringing the stone all the way down, or reversing the materials and putting stone on the bottom and stucco on the top would resolve this problem.

Examples of Heavy Materials

Stone

Brick

Concrete

Examples of Lightweight Materials

Siding

Wood

Stucco

What to **Build**

The materials in this house are used correctly according to their weight. The rusticated stone serves as a base to this two-story residence and easily supports the lightweight stucco and metal roof above.

Fooling the Eye

What Not to Build

In certain applications, brick can be visually inappropriate. In this case, each brick is very noticeable due to the strong color in the gable ends. The shape of the brick and the differences in color of the materials tend to make the elevation appear boxy. Because this house has a smaller primary mass, the use of siding would stretch the visual width. In addition, the use of a solid color would direct the eye to the whole elevation and create an overall larger look.

What to Build

This home, although similar to the one above, appears larger because it is viewed as a whole. When you have a smaller house, material flow is especially important. Here, the uses of multiple materials, textures, and colors are consistent with good design logic. Brick is only used at the foundation or as a base to the house and columns. White painted wood is used for trim and vertical elements, such as the columns and rail posts. Purple-colored shakes cover the gable ends and gray siding is on the walls. The plum-colored door maintains the color scheme and serves as an accent. The viewer automatically responds positively to this well-conceived and consistent design.

CHAPTER 7

Exterior Ornamentation

Not Just a Pretty Face

Exterior ornamentation enhances an overall design. It is an architectural embellishment, an added detail that can serve both functional and aesthetic purposes. However, misguided application of these design elements can detract from the exterior elevation of a home.

Historically, ornamentation has been associated with wealth. The homes of the wealthy usually included a conscious display of ornamentation. Not until the twentieth century did the lack of ornament become popular as a more "honest" expression of structure, material, and function. As design evolved in the 50's and 60's, ornamentation became categorized as decoration, with the stigma of being a lesser component of design.

Decorative elements generally have a practical purpose, although sometimes they can be used to create a theme. Ornamentation may be an integral part of the building—for example, a keystone that is both decorative and a structural component or an attractive balcony railing used for safety. Ornamentation is out of place, or false, when it does not appear functional—for example, shutters should be able to cover the windows when closed or a balcony projection should have doors behind it rather than windows.

Ornamentation is not a fundamental design principle, but is part of the overall design. The concept behind ornamentation is simple and logical: it is a matter of function and thematic design, not simply personal taste. Elements to keep in mind when using ornamentation include:

- Ornamentation that enhances a design element should be shaped and sized to fit that element.

- False ornamentation should appear as if it is functional.

- Items that appear to be part of the structure of the house, such as columns, should function or appear to function as a supporting element.

- Ornamental pieces should be integrated into their surroundings and not appear "tacked on."

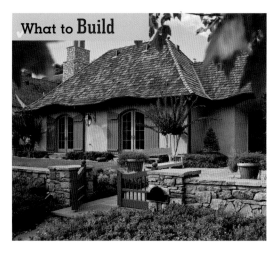

What to Build

These shutters are sized and shaped to cover the doors when closed and provide protection from the elements.

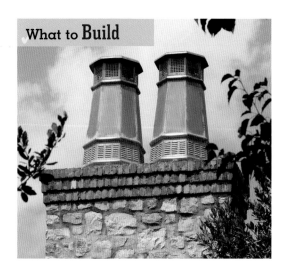

What to Build

Ornate chimney pots are a perfect example of functional ornamentation.

What Not to Build

This wall has enough animation in the variegated stone and does not need the inoperable shutter. The addition of a fabricated object litters the wall and has no purpose. A better way to break up the mass would be to add a trellis with a flowering vine.

✓ What to Build

In this house the ornamentation has purpose and is functional. The doors open onto a true balcony; the lintel above the door supports the structure above; and the roof supports add to the rustic feel of the home.

The Ultra Faux Balcony

This is the ultimate faux balcony. It is large, without access, and not structurally sound enough to hold weight due to the lack of floor joists spanning between the cantilevered beams. The lack of balusters gives the viewer an unsettling feeling. Not only is it non-functional, it lacks elements that would help it visually balance the front elevation.

The token railing provides a false sense of security.

Install a railing and post system.

There is no access to the balcony.

New door provides access to the balcony.

What Not to Build

There are no floor joists to support the balcony.

Add structural supports to make the balcony appear realistic.

The shutter size is incorrect.

Correct the shutter size.

✓ What to **Build**

Construction of a real balcony with new columns corrects proportions and automatically balances the facade. Shutters have been either corrected or removed. The addition of a door allows for access to the balcony, while the addition of railings and floor lines creates a safe and structurally sound balcony. The ornamentation on this home now has purpose.

Architect's
Notebook

CORRECT COLUMNS
WIDER PROPORTIONS

ADD SHUTTERS

INSTALL DOOR

REMOVE SHUTTERS

INCREASE WIDTH OF
SHUTTERS TO COVER
WINDOW

ADD BALUSTERS
4" SPACING

INSTALL FASCIA
OVER FLOOR JOISTS

REMOVE SHUTTERS

REMOVE
SHUTTERS
ADD WINDOW
TRIM

Materials Mix-Up

The wood planking shown on the right side of this home is an illogical form of ornamentation. If its purpose were to represent shutters on a window, they would obviously be nonfunctional. If this was intended to be a door, the frame is trimmed as a window. The next miscue involves the shutters, which are too small to fit the window and be functional, or at least appear functional. Lastly, all of the window surrounds should be made from the same material.

Brick should not be used for trim, frieze board, or window frames.

Remove brick trim where inappropriate.

The shutter size is incorrect.

Correct the shutter sizes so that they appear to function correctly.

What **Not** to Build

The wainscot cuts off the entry surround.

A full-wall plane of stone balances the entry feature.

This wooden ornament serves no purpose.

Leaving this wall blank is better than having a false feature.

✓ What to Build

The subtle changes in material and trim help to unify the elevation. Note the change to the entry surround. As a further improvement, planting a tree on the right side of the home will create a visual break in the blank wall.

DESIGN 101

Faux Facade

The examples of false ornamentation have progressively increased in scale, from the faux shutter to faux balcony to faux porch, and culminating with the faux facade as shown here. Disregarding good design principles, many houses have front veneers that change abruptly.

The front facade of this home gives a good impression that is lost once you turn the corner. The brick facing dies into the window on the side, adding insult to injury.

Shutter Madness

The faux shutters applied to these picture windows are functionally and aesthetically incorrect. Avoid placing shutters on picture windows because making them wide enough to cover the window is impractical.

What Not to Build

⊘ Large picture windows dominate gable-end facade.

✓ Divide large windows into smaller units for better balance.

⊘ Shutters should not be used on picture windows.

✓ Remove shutters from all picture windows.

DESIGN 101

Lack of Support

Use columns as a structural feature to support weight. These clearly tacked on pilasters appear as though they are suspended and weightless. Their placement gives the illusion that the bottom window extends beneath the floor line. The brick support below the column is recessed and adds to the illogical design. When ornamental applications detract from a home, they should be left off. This is another great example of "less is more."

✔ What to **Build**

The use of shutters enhances this home, but it is necessary to divide the picture windows under the gable into smaller units to allow for the correct application of shutters. Removing the shutters on the window on the right side of the lower level allows for the use of the large window. The size of the upper-right window allows for shutters, but in order for the shutters to work in the design, they should be widened and placed on the trim. The small upper window shutters can remain their current size if placed on top of the trim.

DESIGN 101

Window Ornamentation
Making Sense out of Shutters

Windows are often embellished with shutters, special trim, and the like. Historically, shutters were used as protection from the elements and unwanted intruders. Today they are usually applied for decoration and are rarely used to cover windows.

When shutters are used for decoration, it is still important to size and place them to appear as though they would cover the intended window. Although the shutters may not be operable, adding hardware such as strap hinges or shutter dogs gives an authentic feel. Following these simple guidelines will ensure that your shutters look real:

- Shutters should fit over the window.

- Never place shutters outside or set back from the window trim.

- Use shutters that complement the color scheme and the style of the elevation.

What to Build

These shutters are not operable, but they look as though they would cover the entire window if closed. The rough wood complements the rustic stone wall.

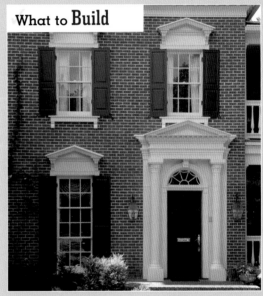

What to Build

These painted shutters follow all the guidelines. They are clearly operable because they have all the necessary hardware, and the window behind them opens.

What to Build

These shutters are shaped and placed correctly on the inside of the brick and would cover the arched opening if closed.

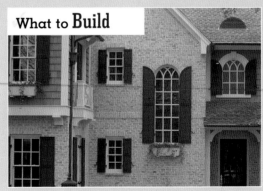

What to Build

These perfectly sized and arched shutters have hinges and shutter dogs that give the window an authentic appearance.

What **Not** to Build

Although these false shutters are the correct size and shape, they are placed so far outside the brick trim they appear as if they are floating on the wall.

What **Not** to Build

Although the shutters are placed correctly, they are disproportionate to the window and appear ridiculous when closed.

What **Not** to Build

This is an incorrect application of single shutters. Shutters should not be used on these windows because they are so close together that there is not enough room between them to create appropriately sized shutters.

What **Not** to Build

The shutters are set back from the window trim and are too small. When shutters are used for decoration, they should still be placed inside the window trim.

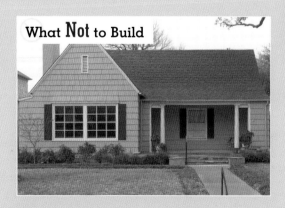

What **Not** to Build

Using single-sized shutters on a double window is an obvious example of falsely applied ornamentation.

DESIGN 101

Window Ornamentation
Lessons in Lintels

A lintel, often referred to as a header when above a window or door, is a structural element integrated in the wall that can be seen on the outside elevation of a home. It is used to support the weight above and must be composed of a sturdy material such as wood, stone, or steel.

Lintels are often falsely applied and appear "tacked on" because they are made of the wrong material, or they are placed incorrectly. When using a material to create an authentic appearing lentil, the material must be integrated into the wall so that it appears to be a part of the wall and provide structural support to the wall above.

This false lentil is not structural because it is tacked on and curved. The concrete element does not even span the width of the window.

What to Build

The lentils above these clerestory windows add character to the upper wall.

What Not to Build

Although the false lentil is flat and spans the width of the window, it is constructed of individual sections and does not appear to function as a supporting element.

Window Ornamentation
Dress it Up with Window Boxes

Window boxes are an excellent design element to use as an ornamental feature. They cast shadow lines and add seasonal color for interest. Certain house styles, such as cottage, country, French, English, and urban, often contain window boxes.

Selecting boxes that are the correct size and proportion to the window is the first step in getting the design right. Window boxes should span the width of the window and be at least 10 inches deep.

There are many material options for window boxes. Formal materials, such as terra-cotta, limestone, and iron, are often complementary to homes that consist of stone. The use of wood as a construction material allows for the window box to be applied to a variation of home styles, but the wood should be durable and rot-resistant. California redwood and cedar fall into this category. If your home is constructed with siding, painted wood or less expensive durable plastic may be an option.

What Not to Build

This box is out of proportion with the window and is false because the window behind it does not open. The box appears to be a misplaced ledge rather than a functional element.

What to Build

This usable window box is correctly sized for the window. The windows are operational.

Stone Work that Doesn't Work

Both the mixture of materials and the multiple levels of wainscoting distort the proportions of the elevation. The ornamental safety railing is too large. Lastly, the entry feature is disrupted by the brick trim and distorted by the large oriel.

The window guard is too large.

✓ Remove the guard, and standardize window trim treatment.

The brick disrupts the entry plane.

✓ Remove brick trim. Stone now defines the entry element.

What **Not** to Build

The stone cuts the wall in half, negating the secondary mass.

✓ Change the stone to brick. The stone is at correct height and forms a base.

The oriel is oversized.

✓ Replace the oriel with a correctly scaled window.

DESIGN 101

All the Right Reasons

The correctly proportioned ornamentation follows a design logic. Repeated pediments throughout the front facade are in proportion to the elements they detail. The corbels below the window pediments are the correct size and scale. The shutters are functional and their color complements the home. The columns add to the hierarchy of the front door.

✓ What to Build

Correcting the material proportions; replacing the over-scaled oriel; removing false ornamentation; and repeating elements, such as trim, found elsewhere on the facade all help to create a more harmonious elevation.

Patchwork Ornamentation

The stone poking through the brick is visually chaotic, dominates the elevation, and detracts from this well-balanced home. The shutters on this home are not quite wide enough to fit the windows. They are a nice detail that is lost among all the patchy stone.

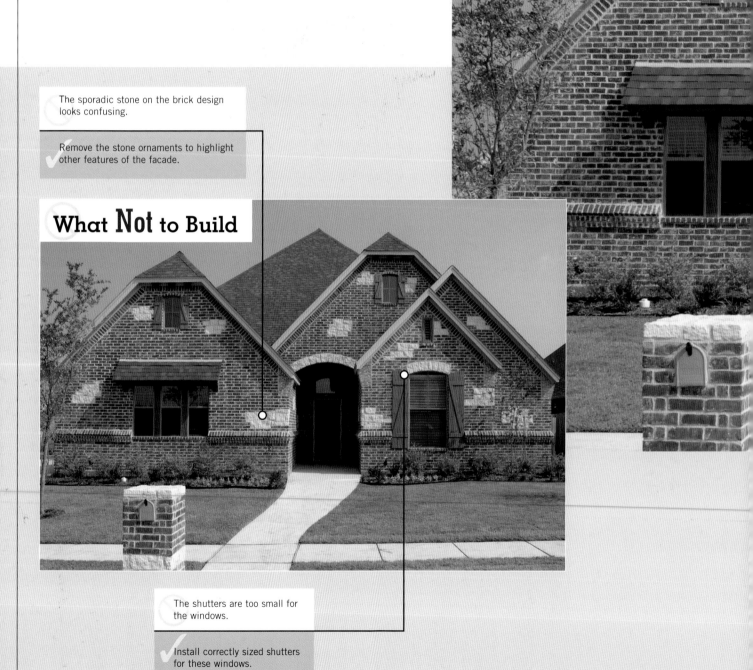

The sporadic stone on the brick design looks confusing.

Remove the stone ornaments to highlight other features of the facade.

What **Not** to Build

The shutters are too small for the windows.

Install correctly sized shutters for these windows.

✔ What to Build

Removing the patchy stone allows for the appreciation of the other features on this home, such as the stone above the windows and the brick detailing which casts a shadow line, depicting an implied wainscot. The corrected shutter size allows the shutters to be more effective as a decorative detail.

DESIGN 101

Correct Use of Keystones

Correct: This keystone is placed correctly at the midsection of the window curve. It serves both a decorative and structural purpose.

Incorrect: These windows do not require a keystone for structural purposes, nor do they work as decorative elements.

A Wacky Elevation

This home is a gross exaggeration of false ornamentation. The false roof above the garage is not covering anything and is clearly tacked on. The shutters over the windows need to be enlarged. The keystones above the garage are obviously false. Keystones are actual structural components that allow an arch to span an opening. Because the proportions of this home are imbalanced, the mixtures of materials further exaggerate the inherent problems.

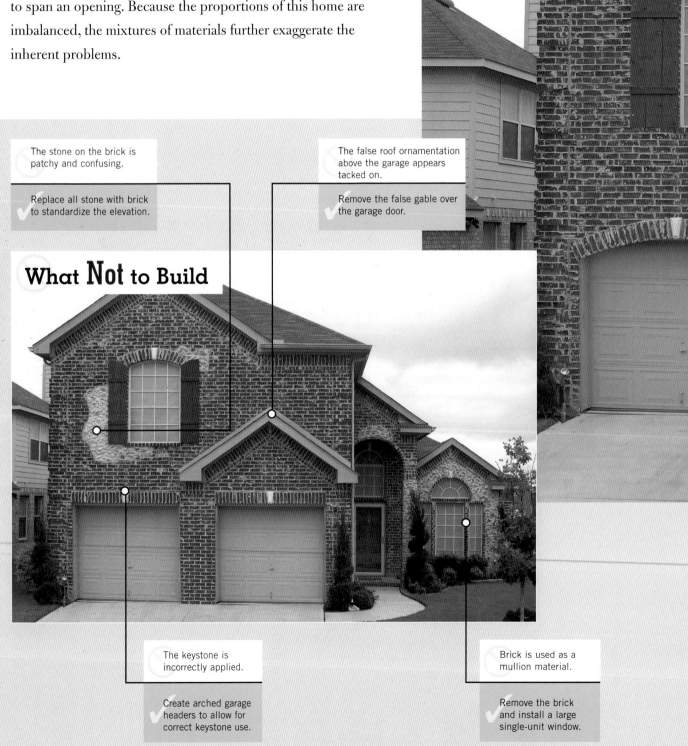

The stone on the brick is patchy and confusing.

✓ Replace all stone with brick to standardize the elevation.

The false roof ornamentation above the garage appears tacked on.

✓ Remove the false gable over the garage door.

What **Not** to Build

The keystone is incorrectly applied.

✓ Create arched garage headers to allow for correct keystone use.

Brick is used as a mullion material.

✓ Remove the brick and install a large single-unit window.

✓ What to **Build**

Although there are still proportion and balance problems with this home, the elevation improves by integrating the garage doors, removing the faux stone, removing the false roof, resizing the shutters, and adding clerestory windows to break up the mass above the garage door. The stone on the right side of the house has been removed and replaced with brick.

Architect's Notebook

INCREASE WIDTH OF SHUTTERS TO COVER WINDOWS

TWO CLERESTORY WINDOWS IN CLOSET

USE THIS ROWLOCK AT GARAGES

ELIMINATE PATCHY STONE—USE BRICK

ELIMINATE PATCHY STONE—USE BRICK
KEYSTONE

BRICK COLUMN—WIDER

WINDOW ASSEMBLY NO BRICK JAMBS

DESIGN 101

Correct Ornamentation

As is the case with other design elements, the use of ornamentation on a home should follow a design logic. Components that normally have a structural function, such as columns, should appear to be fulfilling that function even if they have no structural use on the building at hand. Even if ornamentation is for decoration only, follow the principles of scale, proportion, and balance for correct application.

Maintaining Balance

This ornamentation is both functional and compatible with the design of the home. The railing frames the entry on the first floor while serving the purpose of safety on the second. The squares on the dentil trim, eaves, and frieze are echoed in the design of the balusters.

- **The rail has a safety function.**
- **This rail functions aesthetically as a base to the entry element.**
- **The square motif is repeated throughout the facade.**

Set in Stone

The stone surrounds become a vertical design element. The carved stone is a nice detail that is repeated across the front elevation. Added embellishment in the form of corbels emphasizes the hierarchy of the entry. This is reinforced by the ornate door, which confirms the uniqueness of the home.

- Carved stone is consistently applied.
- The arch form is applied as a theme.
- Corbel embellishments emphasize the importance of the entry.
- The ornate door expresses individuality.

Sensational Siding

The wall and gable end are the same color, yet the smaller scale and texture of the siding on the gable highlights this area as a separate design element. The fish-scale siding mimics the roof pattern and creates a theme for the upper portion of the house. The shutters are correctly proportioned for the window opening.

- The half-timber trim repeats the triangular form.
- The scale and texture of the siding pattern outlines the gable.
- Both the roof and the siding use the same fish-scale pattern.
- Even through they are the same color, the texture of the materials differentiates the gable from the wall.

Subtle Touches

Properly executed ornamentation is often the result of small details. In this case, the paired rafter ends provide a subtle animation and rhythm across the front elevation. They are also a historically accurate detail for this recently constructed craftsman-style example.

- The exposed rafter ends provide a rhythm that moves across the facade.
- The columns match the style of the house and support the roof.

More Than Shelter

Roofs do more than keep out the rain, they are also an important design element of a house. The roof ties together all of the pieces of a home so that they present themselves as one unified space. As a symbol of shelter, the roof may also extend to those areas outside the home that are also livable, such as a porch.

Although the roof pitch is often associated with the style of the house, the roof-to-wall proportions play an important role in the overall aesthetics of a home. The right roof pitch is important to a balanced facade and is often determined by climate, style, or the dimensions of the home it protects.

Most people associate a gable shape with the word roof, but there are a variety of shapes. The most common of these are flat, gable, hipped, and shed. Other shapes that are seen less frequently, or that are subject to regional influences, are gambrel (Dutch gable), mansard, saltbox, and A-frame. A roof type may be driven by the regional climate in which the home is built. Homes built in a climate that experiences heavy snowfall will have steeper slopes than homes built in warmer climates. Particular roof shapes are also identifiable with specific architectural styles.

Materials that cover the roof are just as important as the shapes that compose it. Material weight, color, and texture are all important considerations when choosing a roofing material. Once the material has been chosen, the color should complement the colors of the home. The key elements for good roof design include:

- Avoid using more than two roof shapes.

- Using a simple roof shape can reinforce the visual order of the facade below.

- Use roofs to extend living spaces, such as the roof over a porch.

- The roof's color should complement the elevation.

- The flow of the rooflines should always go from high to low.

What to Build

The classic gable roof is a common roof shape found on many homes.

What Not to Build

When a residence has a flat roof, the wall is the aesthetic focus. The application of roofing material as siding is an attempt to transform the wall into a roof. Conversely, on the right side, the roof is pretending to be a wall, resulting in visual confusion.

The mixture of roof shapes and the interruption of the rooflines create an unnecessarily complicated design.

The hip (top) and shed (bottom) roof shapes are well balanced and proportioned on this symmetrical home.

Too Large for Comfort

The constant slope of this steeply pitched roof creates a mass that is three times the vertical height of the porch. As a result, the roof appears to be "pressing" the first floor into the ground. The conflicting rooflines on the right side of the house are not integrated into the overall design of the home.

An oversized attic creates a roof mass that overwhelms the front elevation.

✓ Create a true second story to break up the roof mass and establish the correct proportions.

What **Not** to Build

The visual weight of the roof compresses the perceived height of the first floor.

✓ A shallow-pitched roof forms a horizontal line and creates an image typical of ranch-style homes.

Conflicting rooflines do not flow with each other or the main roof.

✓ Simplified rooflines are visually pleasing.

✓ What to **Build**

Creating a roofline for the porch and turning the attic space into a second story shrunk the overwhelming roof mass. The solution shown creates the horizontal lines associated with a ranch-style home. The rooflines of the right side of the home are now integrated into the rest of the elevation.

Architect's Notebook

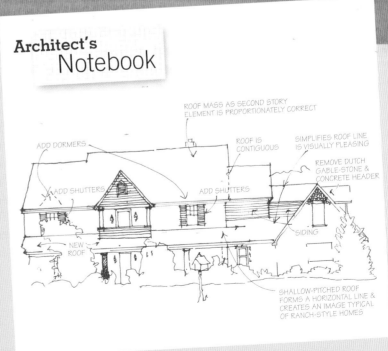

ROOF MASS AS SECOND STORY ELEMENT IS PROPORTIONATELY CORRECT

ADD DORMERS

ROOF IS CONTIGUOUS

SIMPLIFIES ROOF LINE IS VISUALLY PLEASING

REMOVE DUTCH GABLE-STONE & CONCRETE HEADER

ADD SHUTTERS

ADD SHUTTERS

SIDING

NEW ROOF

SHALLOW-PITCHED ROOF FORMS A HORIZONTAL LINE & CREATES AN IMAGE TYPICAL OF RANCH-STYLE HOMES

Disconnected Design

The broken roofline visually divides the house into two separate pieces. The single dormer is not enough to balance the tall and bulky chimney, and it appears to get lost on the large roof mass.

The dormer is too small to balance the chimney.

Add extra dormers to balance the chimney.

What **Not** to Build

The broken roof causes the viewer to see two separate masses below.

Create a continuous roof to allow the house to be seen as one piece.

DESIGN 101

Roofing Rhythm

The repetition of rooflines in gable ends can create a sequence of elements that gives rhythm to the design of the home. Roof patterns and the regularity of forms provide an inherent design logic. The observer's response to the predictability of shapes verifies visual order.

✓ What to Build

Moving the porch cover forward to align with the front wall creates a continuous roofline. This gives continuity to the lines of the home and allows it to be seen as a whole. The addition of correctly scaled dormers helps balance the chimney while breaking up the roof mass. Shutter adjustments finish the look and are proportionate to the windows.

Multiple Personalities

The multiple roof shapes break up the visual flow, providing a good example of an over-animated roofline.

✔ What to **Build**

Simplicity in design, and a cohesive roof form to tie it all together, creates a balanced elevation.

This is a good example of how multiple roof shapes (Dutch gable, gable, shed, and hipped) create a confusing roofline.

✔ Simplify the roof line to tie together the secondary masses.

What **Not** to Build

✔ Repeat the gable ends to reinforce the logic of the secondary mass as a projection that consistently intersects the primary mass behind it.

DESIGN101

The Pitch on Roofing

Roof pitch is an important aesthetic aspect of the home. The pitch determines where on the elevation the viewer's eye will focus. This relates to roof/wall proportions that are determined by the degree of slope.

Rule #1 To draw the focus to the wall, allowing it to dominate the facade, use a flat or low-pitched roof. The angle should be less than 30 degrees.

Rule #2 To give equal value to the roof and the wall, use a standard pitch with an angle of 30-45 degrees. This is common in two-story homes.

Rule #3 To allow the roof to dominate the wall (acceptable in specific architectural styles), use a steep pitch with an angle greater than 45 degrees. Although this type is acceptable in A-frame homes, it can cause problems in other designs.

The wall is the main focus of this home. The use of a low-pitched roof is an effective way to draw attention to the details below.

This is an exaggerated example of a steep roof. When there is too much roof, there are no solutions. The techniques of intersecting gables and chimneys do not help offset the massiveness of the roof that overpowers the walls. This is an insurmountable slope.

This standard pitch has equal value in the roof/wall proportions. When this pitch is used, neither the wall nor the roof dominates the elevation. For every 12 feet of horizontal roof, 6 feet of wall should be found below. This home meets the "6:12" ratio often referred to in the building trade.

All Mixed Up

The mixture of roof shapes, including hip, Dutch gable, modified hip, and gable, is visually confusing. The misplaced and oversized oriel above the entry punctuates the roofline and draws your eye upward, detracting from the entry composition.

The oriel is oversized and detracts from the entry.

Remove the oriel and add a gable end. This will reinforce the entry element.

What Not to Build

A modified hip roof adds a fourth roof shape.

A repeated gable end creates rhythm and visual order.

The Dutch gable introduces another roof shape, causing visual distraction where the viewer expects to see repetition of the adjacent gable.

Remove the Dutch gable and add a standard gable.

What to Build

Creating gable ends across the roofline establishes visual order. An increased height at the entry element restores the perceived importance of the front door. Replacing the large oriel with a gable form and louvered vent provides the correct proportions. Simplification of elements such as rooflines and ornamentation creates a harmonious elevation.

DESIGN 101

Coloring the Canopy

Roof color can make a good house great or ruin an otherwise perfect facade. Following a few guidelines will help ensure that the roof color complements the home.

- For the greatest impact, use a contrasting, but complementary, color to the home.

- On a blended roof, an accent color that matches the wall enhances the scheme.

- A darker roof color will ground or lower the volume of the home. This aspect is effective in changing perceived proportions where necessary.

The contrasting color of the clay roof enhances the beauty of the lighter stone.

Overshadowed Entry

The use of a roof that sheds (slopes) down to the entry is another form of "steep pitch roof syndrome." This continuous line creates a mass that is disproportionate to the facade. The visual distortion effectively dwarfs the perceived height of the porch.

This dormer is not enough to offset the large roof.

✓ Add dormers to break up the roof mass.

What Not to Build

This extended, steeply pitched roof creates an oversized roof mass

✓ Place the shed roof at a shallow pitch to better define the porch.

The height of the porch is distorted by the large roof mass.

✓ Create a gable shape to balance the roof mass and establish entry hierarchy.

✓ What to **Build**

The creation of a new roofline that transitions into the roof beyond, as well as the addition of the pediment, gives visual height to the entry. An additional dormer completes the effort to balance the primary roof mass. The orientation of the roof shapes plays a key role in the impact of the street elevation.

DESIGN 101

The Habitable Attic

Massive roofs are often a missed opportunity for habitable space. In some instances, where building up is a better option than building out, partial attic space can become a game room or a much-needed home office. The foundation and roof are already in place, so the expansion of space focuses mostly on any necessary additional framing. In the house shown here, a mansard roof helps expand the attic space. Other roofing styles that can accommodate increased living space include shed, gambrel, and gable dormers.

DESIGN 101

Righteous Roofs

In many houses, the roof can overwhelm the entire facade. To prevent that from happening, it is important that the roof mass be balanced so that the scale of the roof and its proportion are as pleasing as the rest of the front elevation. A well-designed roof should be an integral part of the overall design of the house.

Asymmetrical Balance

In the roof-wall relationship, a steep-pitched roof can easily dominate the wall below. As the roof angle increases, the roof moves toward the observer and visually becomes more wall-like. This trait is exaggerated by a uniformity of color that creates a mass that overwhelms the elevation. Intersecting gables negate the primary mass of this home, and a potentially overbearing secondary mass is offset by the placement of two dormers. The result is a house with a very steep-pitched roof that has achieved asymmetrical balance. The roof color complements the dark gray accents in the brick.

- Intersecting gable ends break up the primary roof mass.
- Dormers offset the secondary mass.

Personality Plus

The roof seems to flow seamlessly over the home. By incorporating chimneys, the gable ends are given additional prominence. An arch interrupts the central roof over the door, drawing attention to the front entry. This subtle expression is repeated in the rounded arch door and allows the surround to be articulated with a raised pediment. This comprehensive scheme is completed with the use of accent roof tiles that match the peach brick color. The result is a home that utilizes minimal details to create personality.

- The accent roof tiles match the coloring in the brick.
- The two chimneys enhance the gable ends.
- An undulating arched roof brings focus to the entry.

Informal Appeal

Two roof types are evident in this example: gable and shed. A steep-pitched gable forms the main roof. A shallow-pitched shed creates a horizontal line that provides visual order to the full width of the porch. Repeating the shed at the large dormer reinforces the horizontal lines of the design and breaks up the massive roof beyond. This is an excellent composition utilizing multiple roof shapes.

- A shed roof dormer repeats the linear theme and breaks up the roof mass beyond.

- The shed roof provides a horizontal line that gives visual order to the porch.

Balanced Roof Elements

The roof mass is effectively broken up through the use of correctly scaled dormers. The dormers add light to the second level and help balance the front facade. This is also an excellent example of an integrated porch that utilizes the main roof to form the porch covering.

- The main roof pitch continues down to form the porch covering.

- The balanced roof mass creates the correct scale for the porch roof. It appears to support the roof above.

- The dormers break up the roof mass.

Interesting Shapes

This is an excellent example of a roof form utilizing intersecting shapes. In this case, it is the gable ends that project from the main hipped roof. This technique allows the primary focus to be shared between the front door and the stained-glass window to the right. The scale of the two gable shapes nicely balances the primary mass of the main roof.

- Projecting gable ends provide balance to the primary mass of the main roof.

- The gable shape brings focus to the front door and the adjacent living space.

CHAPTER 9

Dormers

Letting in the Light

Dormers are "pint-sized" structures with walls, roofs, and windows that interrupt rooflines and slopes. They provide light and ventilation to attics or top-story living spaces. Dormers add curb appeal and are a great aesthetic addition to the exterior elevation. Because they project from the roof mass and are so conspicuous, it is important that they are scaled and placed correctly.

The word "dormer" originates from the French word *dormir,* which means "to sleep." It can be traced back to the French architect Francois Mansart (1598-1666), who gave us the mansard-style roof. Mansart created his dormers to get around building height limitations in Paris. His solution was a four-sided roof with very steeply pitched, almost vertical, slopes. He placed a series of windows or "dormers" in the steeper pitched portion of this new roof concept to allow in light and fresh air.

Dormers have a multifaceted role, depending on their number, size, and placement, in determining the aesthetic outcome of an architectural design. Sizing and scaling dormers so that they are in proportion to the surrounding roof mass is crucial. When using multiple dormers, their placement and spacing becomes important. Key aspects in the effective use of dormers include:

- Place the dormers to align vertically with windows below to create visual order.

- Use the correct size so that the scale is proportionate to the mass of the main roof.

- Avoid dormers that are oversized or placed too high because they can obstruct the main roof ridgeline.

- Evenly space multiple dormers to create a rhythm, which balances the facade.

- Dormers are attic windows. At least 75 percent of the dormer face should be glazing.

- Use the same materials for the dormers that are used elsewhere on the elevation.

What to Build

These equally spaced dormers are vertically aligned with the door and columns below.

What to Build

The dormers on this mansard roof provide additional living space.

What to Build

Pedimented dormers are often found on Georgian, Federal, and Colonial Revival homes.

What to Build

The dormer allows for the addition of a bonus room or study to this otherwise one-story home.

Too Many Dormers

The street view of this house shouts "dormers." The additional dormers that have been crammed into the left side of the house are out of place. Although the building code would require some type of window here, dormers are not the answer. The triple dormers above the entry are proportionately correct, yet the color makes them appear oversized.

The color of these dormers makes them appear too large.

Change the color to complement the first-floor color scheme.

What **Not** to Build

These dormers appear crammed into this space.

Remove the dormers and create a wall with windows.

✓ What to **Build**

The second-story space now includes a wall and windows that balance the facade and meet fire code requirements. The color of the remaining dormers now complements the stone below, and they no longer appear oversized.

Architect's Notebook

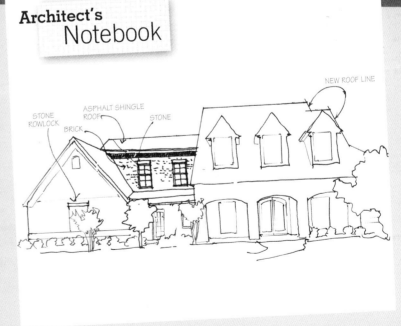

STONE ROWLOCK

BRICK

ASPHALT SHINGLE ROOF

STONE

NEW ROOF LINE

Curves That Don't Work

The arched roof dormer and the wall dormer introduce a third roof shape that is out of context with this pseudo-Tudor style home. The arched form, in tandem with the expansive wall surface, competes with the entry.

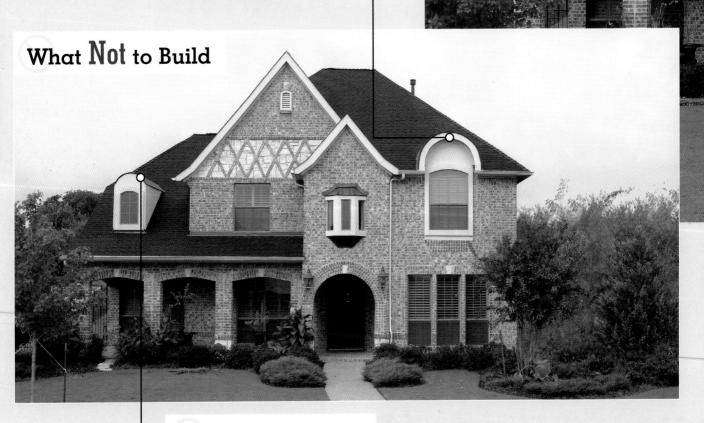

This oversized wall dormer competes with the entry.

✓ Remove the wall dormer and replace it with a window.

What Not to Build

This curvilinear roof shape is inappropriate for the style of the house.

✓ Turn the dormer into a gable shape to make it more appropriate to the house.

✓ What to **Build**

Repeating a gable roof on the far left dormer and deleting the arched roof dormer unifies the roofline. This also corrects the competition between the front door and the wall dormer, turning the focus back to the entry.

DESIGN 101

Locating Dormers

The placement of this dormer allows the maximum amount of sunlight into the central space of the home. Aesthetically, this "centricity" balances the elevation while aligning with the columns below to produce an implied entry feature that focuses on the front door. The scheme is completed with a finishing touch that repeats the open-end rafter detail that typifies a craftsman-style bungalow.

The Afterthought

This token dormer is incorrectly placed and is unable to compete proportionately with the roof mass. It is not necessary for interest or any aesthetic reason, because the straightforward design is well balanced with simple lines.

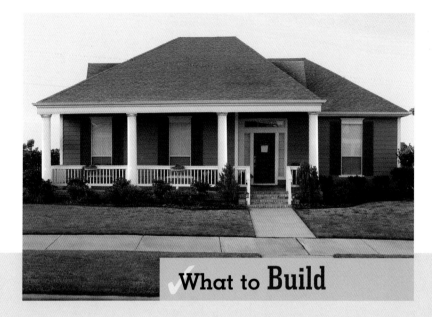

✓ What to Build

Placing two dormers, one on each side of the hipped roof, allows light in without distracting from the front elevation.

The dormer is out of place and disproportionate to the main roof.

Remove it but add side dormers to admit natural light.

What **Not** to Build

Size Adjustment

The out-of-scale dormers are disproportionate to the roof mass and do not match the style of the home. The stick-like columns are too narrow, and the false shutters are incorrectly sized and placed outside the trim.

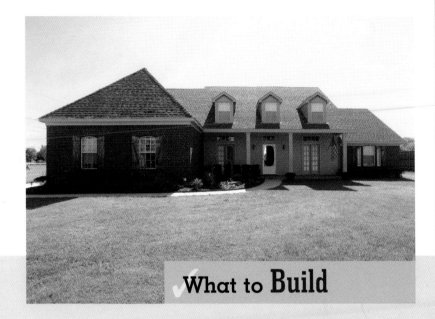

What to **Build**

Gable dormers are more suitable for this country-style home. The gable aligns with the space between the columns and unifies the right side of the elevation while balancing the secondary mass projection on the left.

This dormer roof type is not consistent with the style of the home.

✔ Add gable dormers to better suit the ranch style of the house.

What **Not** to Build

These dormers are too small.

✔ Correct dormer size to make them proportionate to the roof mass.

Dormers Steal the Focus

These dormers are much too tall. In fact, they appear taller than the height of the porch roof, detracting from the front entry area. Instead of offsetting the secondary mass of the roof, the dormers are the focal point of the elevation.

These oversized dormers are disproportionate to the roof mass and dwarf the entry below.

✓ Replace with dormers that are the correct size for this roof.

What **Not** to Build

This amount of siding emphasizes the size of the dormers.

✓ Increase the amount of glazing.

✓ What to Build

Correctly scaled dormers are proportionate to the secondary mass and balance this symmetrical design. The dormers no longer dwarf the entry below. The glass-to-siding ratio on the dormers is more consistent with accepted design practices.

DESIGN 101

Wall Dormers

This is an excellent example of a wall dormer that places the window in the same plane as the wall below. The flush face of the dormer becomes a vertical extension of the wall line. Detailed ornamental surrounds are a trait of wall dormers. This feature is necessary to visually cap the wall element because the dormer roof is barely visible. The placement of these arched dormers creates a symmetrically balanced facade.

The 75-Percent Test

Dormers can enhance an exterior elevation if the materials and size are correct. The 75-percent rule states that the glass, also called glazing, should occupy at least 75 percent of the front surface of a dormer. Even though the overall dormer may be proportionate to the roof mass, using a smaller percentage of glass may cause the dormer to appear heavy and out of scale with the first floor.

FAIL: The Lilliputian shutters magnify the large amount of siding on this dormer. The glazing is less than 75 percent.

PASS: This home uses the correct amount of glazing. The eyebrow shape of the windows is echoed in the dormers' roofline.

PASS: The decorative curve of the dormers frames the correct ratio of glazing on each.

PASS: These shed dormers clearly follow the 75-percent rule of glazing and allow for the maximum amount of light.

FAIL: Although the shutters take up some of the visual volume of the siding because of their contrasting color, the glazing is far below the 75-percent rule.

PASS: The white trim provides contrast to the gray siding, but the glazing does not follow the 75-percent rule.

FAIL: The glazing is less than 75 percent, making the siding the dominant material.

False Appearance

These oversized dormers are ineffective in breaking up the roof mass. The false shutters draw further attention to the dormers, which dominate the elevation.

These dormers are out of scale with the home.

Replace two large dormers with three correctly sized structures.

The glazing is less than 75 percent.

Correctly sized dormers contain the right amount of glass.

What Not to Build

The false shutters are incorrectly applied.

Remove shutters.

DESIGN 101

Logical Design

In this example, the dormers maximize attic space and complement the front facade. Often, the relationship between the dormers and the wall below is ignored. In this case, the dormers' alignment with the windows below integrates them into the elevation and visually anchors each end of the home. The gabled dormers match the style of the house, and the repetition provides a logical order that balances the interesting variety of rooflines.

✓ What to **Build**

Even though an additional dormer
has been added, the three dormers together balance the facade without creating a top-heavy appearance.

Pasted-On Dormers

These false wall dormers appear "pasted" onto the wall. Correctly used wall dormers intersect with the roof and are an extension of the wall plane, as seen on the left side of the elevation.

Dormers intersect the walls, not the roof, of this house.

✓ Remove dormer shapes and replace with windows.

What Not to Build

✓ This is a correct use of dormers.

The pasted-on wall dormer distracts from the entry.

✓ New windows admit sunlight and balance the mass without detracting from the entry.

✓ What to **Build**

By replacing the wall dormers with windows, the entry becomes the main focus of the facade of this house.

Architect's Notebook

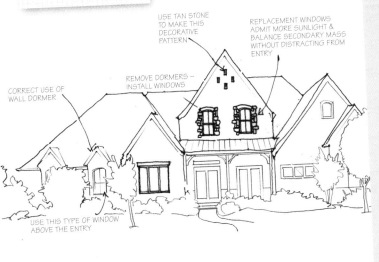

USE TAN STONE TO MAKE THIS DECORATIVE PATTERN

REPLACEMENT WINDOWS ADMIT MORE SUNLIGHT & BALANCE SECONDARY MASS WITHOUT DISTRACTING FROM ENTRY

REMOVE DORMERS – INSTALL WINDOWS

CORRECT USE OF WALL DORMER

USE THIS TYPE OF WINDOW ABOVE THE ENTRY

CHAPTER 10

Proportion and Balance

Partners in Design

Throughout this book, we have shown how the fundamental rules of architecture govern the individual parts of a house. Combining these parts in the proper way creates good design. But that is the main sticking point of architecture: if strict rules regulate how the parts of a house go together, all houses will be monotonous and boring. However, if there is no organizing principle to guide in selecting and combining parts, all houses will be visually chaotic. That is where an understanding of proportions comes in. Understanding proportions is not about solving a mathematical equation, but about becoming familiar with what proportions are aesthetically pleasing.

To help you do that, we are going to show you photos of correctly proportioned houses so that you build up a familiarity with pleasing proportions. How many times have you thought "I'll know it when I see it?" This chapter will help you know it when you see it.

Balance works in concert with proportion. A symmetrically balanced home will have two matching sides when it is divided down the middle. An asymmetrical design will not have matching halves, but the visual weight of the sections will be comparatively equal. Visual weight is a combination of factors, including shape, mass, proportion, and sometimes color. Key aspects in using balance and proportion in design include:

- Use dormers to break up a roof mass and balance the facade.

- On two-story homes, the vertical alignment of windows instills a design logic that creates visual order and helps balance the elevation.

- Beltlines create a visual break, which alters the proportions of the elevation.

- To create asymmetrical balance, arrange different shapes with equal visual weight.

- Applying materials in a consistent manner helps balance an elevation.

What to Build

The correctly proportioned elements on this home work together to create a harmonious design that is asymmetrically balanced from left to right and top to bottom. The protruding secondary mass on the right visually balances the rest of the facade. The two well-placed dormers offset the large roof mass. The small covered entry ties the elevation elements together and reinforces the entry hierachy.

What to **Build**

Symmetry is expressed with height variations in the front wall plane. The larger gable ends on either side of this home are sized to the volume of the living space behind. The entry gable is smaller and centers the human-scaled foyer.

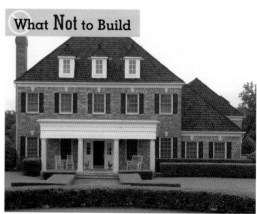

What **Not** to Build

The oversized entablature, which is disproportionate to the facade behind, throws this symmetrical home off balance. The columns that support the entablature are lower than the first-story windows. By scaling down the depth of the entablature, the column height can be raised and the problem resolved.

A Too-Tall Gable

From left to right, this house is symmetrically balanced. However, the entry disrupts the proportions of this home. It is much too tall and soars over the main roof.

The entry element is oversized.

Reduce the size of the entry gable to make it proportionate to the facade.

What **Not** to Build

The shutters do not fit on the window frame.

✓ Remove the shutters.

Add lighting and vent to complete the entry element.

DESIGN 101

Color Balance

This home is balanced from left to right and from top to bottom. Not only do the shutters on the wall balance the roof mass, their blue color offsets the gray roof and gives visual balance to the overall facade.

✔ What to Build

The entry gable is now in proportion to the rest of the roof. The color of the front door draws attention to the entrance. Lights have been placed on either side of the door, and a vent has been added to fill the gable.

Uneven Sides

The centerline shows that the two-story element creates an imbalance or too much weight on the right-hand side of the house. The mass on the right outweighs the single-story garage.

The two-story element tips the balance of the elevation to the right.

Add a balcony to break up the two-story component and scale down the height.

What Not to Build

The single-story garage is underweight in comparison with the balance of the elevation.

Replace with a gable roof that increases the height of the vertical planes, giving weight to the single-story element.

The horizontal line further reduces the visual height.

✓ What to Build

In order to bring a sense of balance to this home, the left side must be visually raised and the right side must be visually lowered. Placing a gable roof over the garage increases the height of the left side. On the right, the introduction of a balcony at the entry visually lowers the height of this tall element. Although this home's layout negates any ability to achieve true asymmetrical balance, the corrections have improved the imbalanced facade.

Architect's Notebook

MATCH GABLE ON GARAGE.

BALCONY DOORS

GABLE ROOF INSTALL VENT

BRICK

REPLACE "BOX BEAM" WITH ROWLOCK HEADER

CENTER DOOR

Gable Steals the Show

The selection of materials, shapes, and colors can affect the perception of balance even though the size of the mass remains the same. The right-sided gable now overpowers the understated entry. The visual flow is disrupted by the change in colors. The lack of detailing on the wall makes the secondary mass appear even wider than it is. In this house, the choice of materials and roof shape skews the perception of balance.

Gable overpowers the primary mass of the house.

✔ Replace the gable end with a hip roof that will recede into the primary mass beyond.

What **Not** to Build

The color scheme breaks the visual flow.

✔ Complementary color scheme helps to blend elements of the facade together.

Window area dominates the facade, drawing attention away from the entry area.

✔ Simplify the window assembly so that it balances the windows on the porch.

DESIGN 101

Mirror Image

This home is symmetrically balanced and shows a perfect mirror image (including the chimneys) on both sides of an imaginary centerline. A symmetrically balanced home has a more formal appearance than houses that are not symmetrical.

✓ What to Build

Removing the dominant gable and replacing it with a hip roof helps to balance the elevation. This allows the secondary roof mass to blend in with the primary roof behind and keeps the front wall from having too much height. The quoins give the extra visual weight needed to balance the right side of the home. This example uses window trim colors that are very similar and blend to create visual flow.

This Way Up

The gambrel-roofed secondary mass is grossly disproportionate to the rest of the facade. The two-story bay window design contributes to the dominating affect of this portion of the elevation. Other elements, such as an incorrect number of columns and the wall dormer, provide a vertical emphasis that adds to the imbalance of the elevation.

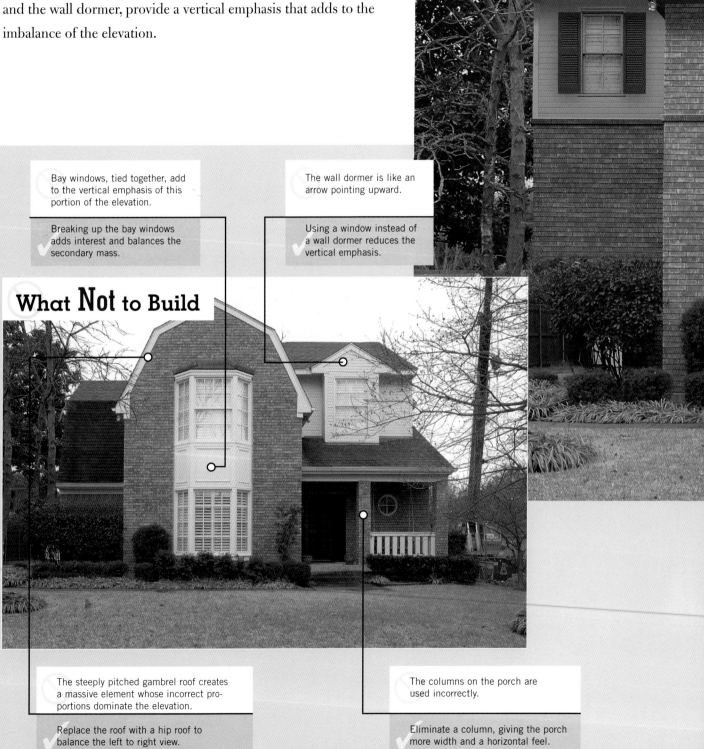

Bay windows, tied together, add to the vertical emphasis of this portion of the elevation.

✓ Breaking up the bay windows adds interest and balances the secondary mass.

The wall dormer is like an arrow pointing upward.

✓ Using a window instead of a wall dormer reduces the vertical emphasis.

What Not to Build

The steeply pitched gambrel roof creates a massive element whose incorrect proportions dominate the elevation.

✓ Replace the roof with a hip roof to balance the left to right view.

The columns on the porch are used incorrectly.

✓ Eliminate a column, giving the porch more width and a horizontal feel.

✓ What to **Build**

Creating a hip roof and breaking up the vertical line of the double bay window with smaller-sized bay windows have reduced the vertical emphasis on the left side of the house. Deleting the dormer and replacing it with a window brings focus back down to the entry. The consistent application of materials—siding on the top and brick on the bottom—creates a design logic that further helps balance the elevation.

Architect's Notebook

CORRECT ROOF LINE ON LEFT WING

HIPPED ROOF

REPLACE DORMER WITH A WALL AND WINDOW

DOUBLE-HUNG WINDOW W/ SHUTTERS

BURGUNDY COLOR SHUTTERS

BELTLINE DARKER BRICK

BELTLINE DARKER BRICK

METAL ROOF

BRICK

REMOVE COLUMN

DESIGN 101

Well-Balanced Designs

Balance and Rhythm

The multiple shapes on this home work together to form a balanced asymmetrical composition. The chimney on the right helps balance that side of the roofline. The left to right progression of height in the gables draws the eye upward to create visual equilibrium.

- Both sides of the house feature a tall chimney.

- The progressive height of the gables draws the eye upward as it moves left to right.

- A larger gable and a chimney anchor the right side.

Turret Balances the Elevation

The turret, which is given added weight by its white trim, balances the higher tower on the left. As the elevation ascends, the window size decreases proportionately. The two windows above the porch roof are proportionate within the wall space. Each element in the design is proportionate to its placement on the elevation, which equates to an asymmetrically balanced facade.

- The turret on the right counterbalances the tower. The white trim adds weight to the turret.

- The windows are sized proportionately to the wall space.

- The change in window size on the tower contributes to the overall balance.

Two Types of Balance

This home is symmetrically balanced. From top to bottom, proportional elements and techniques are composed for asymmetrical balance. A change in materials and an accented beltline create two distinct bands of wall surface. The corbelled balcony beams are repeated in the exposed rafter ends.

- The materials on the bottom part of the wall balance the roof mass.

- Delicate balcony components create an element of focus that assists in offsetting the roof mass.

Proportion is in the Details

Once proportions have been established with the larger masses of the home (primary, secondary, and the roof), they must be addressed in the details that are part of the design. Just like the pieces of a puzzle, the pieces of a home must fit together logically to form the overall design. The principles of Greek architecture remind us that larger pieces should be placed at the lower level as a way to ground the elevation. As the wall extends upward, the components should become smaller. In some instances, such as flat front elevations, the pieces may remain a consistent size.

What to **Build**

These windows decrease in size as they ascend. The lower windows ground the mass, and the top window fits nicely within the gable end.

What **Not** to Build

The smaller window is dwarfed by the larger doors above and is counterintuitive.

What to **Build**

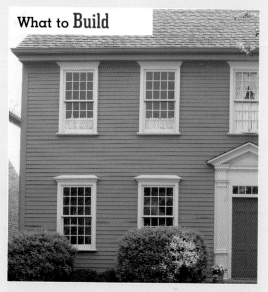

Home styles such as Colonial and Federalist have flat front walls. In these styles, window proportions are generally consistent throughout the elevation.

Split Personality

The placement of materials on this home have caused its otherwise asymmetrical design to appear imbalanced. The division of materials gives this home a "duplex" affect.

Stone kept on the center brings hierarchy to the entry.

What **Not** to Build

Stone and brick divide the home into two halves.

Replace this portion with brick to create asymmetrical balance.

✓ What to **Build**

By rearranging the placement of the veneered materials, the viewer can now appreciate the asymmetrical form of the home. Stone now covers the center element, which is flanked by two brick sides, and the windows have received minor adjustments.

DESIGN 101

Tricky Situations

Asymmetrical balance can be tricky when there is a massive element to one side. In this case, a large chimney to the right is balanced with a taller roof mass on the left that is interrupted by a large projecting window. The combination of elements on either side of the centerline equalizes the visual scale.

DESIGN 101

Knowing It When You See It

These houses are proportionally balanced in all directions. After viewing these examples, you should be able to develop an intuitive sense of what is right. Now when you look at houses, you will know balance and proportion when you see it.

What to **Build**

What to **Build**

What to **Build**

What to **Build**

What to **Build**

These house are either imbalanced or have disproportionate elements. Look through them and see if you can spot the problems— some are fairly obvious. Try to create your own fixes.

What **Not** to Build

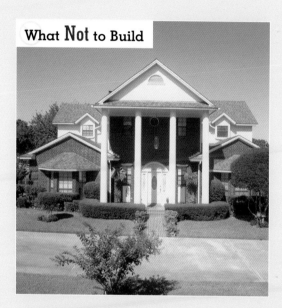

What **Not** to Build

What **Not** to Build

What **Not** to Build

What **Not** to Build

What **Not** to Build

Blending Styles

Architectural styles are intriguing because they often tell us something about the period they represent or the geographic areas from which they come. There are about 25 identifiable American residential styles, although the many regional variations of specific styles make it difficult to conclusively identify a home as a certain style.

Understanding style types and applying the principles of design when building or remodeling will aid you in creating timeless elevations. Knowing the elements of a residential style will help you avoid mixing incompatible features. When you combine architectural elements with no regard for scale or proportion, the result is a hodgepodge of details that form visually chaotic elevations.

From the design perspective, it is not important whether the house is 100 percent true to the "pedigree" of the style or that it has a bit of a "mongrel" in it. What is important is the type and way those elements are combined.

There are two forms of mixed architectural styles. The most common mixture of styles results when a basic style is altered in some fashion. This usually occurs when a house is renovated to add space or modernize the exterior. Renovating to reduce maintenance chores often results in mixing of styles, such as when a homeowner replaces wood shakes or clapboard with vinyl siding. Some key ideas for combining architectural elements include

- Combining elements that are within subtypes of a dominant style to help ensure visual unity.

- Avoiding the mixing architectural styles that do not blend well. A Spanish tile roof will not work on a Craftsman home.

- Researching your home's style to help you make color, texture, and material choices that enhance the facade.

- Keeping scale, balance, and proportion in mind when applying or mixing different stylistic elements on an elevation.

- When using several different styles and forms, using a single color or material to unify the elements.

What Not to Build

This French wall dormer has curves and smooth textures that conflict with the Tudor style.

What to Build

This classic Colonial home has a side gable roof. The double-hung windows, placed five across, and its shallow-molded, unadorned cornice are features consistent with the Adams subtype.

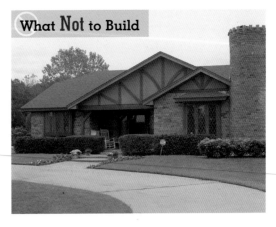

What Not to Build

The half-timbered gables and diamond-pattern windows on this ranch-style home typify the neo-Tudor movement of the 1960s. Although there are elements from three styles, the overwhelming problem is the oversized and dominating chimney. When mixing styles, it is important to consider balance and proportion.

What to Build

The gable detailing with patterned shingles and stained glass is typical of Queen Anne Victorian homes.

Semi-Tudor

The oriel, steeply pitched roof, and prominent gables are all traits of the Tudor style. However, some of the extra details shown here clash with the Tudor traits, including the geometric pattern in the brick above the arched entry and the shed roof over the bay window.

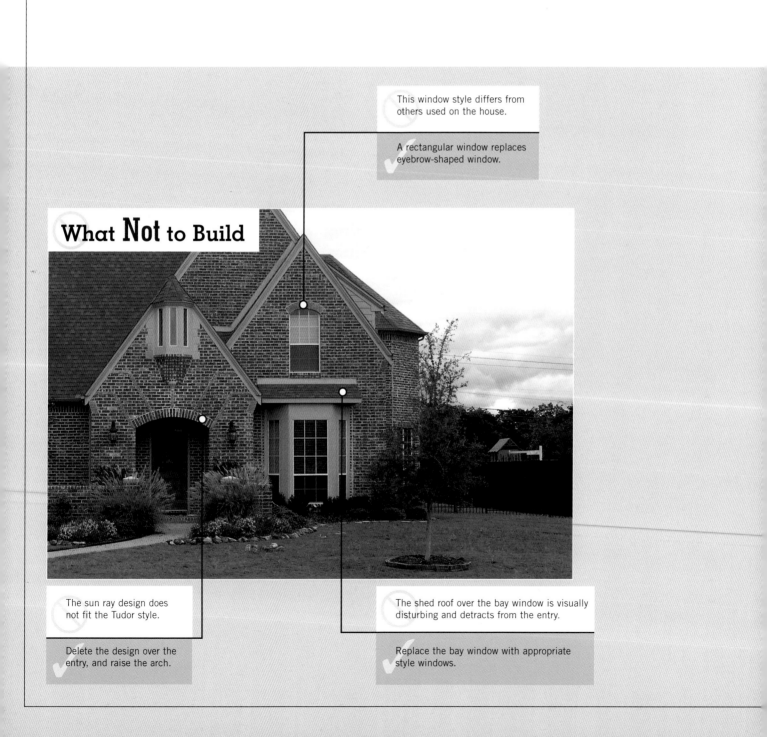

This window style differs from others used on the house.

A rectangular window replaces eyebrow-shaped window.

What **Not** to Build

The sun ray design does not fit the Tudor style.

Delete the design over the entry, and raise the arch.

The shed roof over the bay window is visually disturbing and detracts from the entry.

Replace the bay window with appropriate style windows.

✓ What to **Build**

A bank of rectangular windows replace the stucco bay window with its shed roof. Removing the geometric lines in the brick and raising the entry arch corrects the scale and brings focus to where it belongs. Replacing the curved-top window on the second floor with a rectangular unit ties the two levels together.

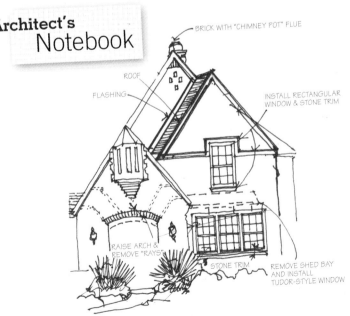

Architect's Notebook

BRICK WITH "CHIMNEY POT" FLUE

ROOF

FLASHING

INSTALL RECTANGULAR WINDOW & STONE TRIM

RAISE ARCH & REMOVE "RAYS"

STONE TRIM

REMOVE SHED BAY AND INSTALL TUDOR-STYLE WINDOW

Spanish Deco

The clay roof and stucco walls exhibit Spanish influence, but the radiating incised lines at the entry introduce an Art Deco geometric motif. The two styles have a conflict of interest and detract from the entry. The second-story windows appear to rest directly on the roof.

The windows die into the roof.

✓ Raise the windows so that a sill is visible.

What **Not** to Build

✓ What to **Build**

The solution here calls for deleting the Art Deco elements. Removing the incised lines and adding corbels creates a seamless approach that complements the style of the home. Raising the second-floor window reveals sills and correct window trim. Repeating details from other parts of the elevation, such as the trim around the windows, ties the entry element into the facade.

The Spanish-style clay roof and stucco walls clash with the geometric design.

✓ Remove the radiating design. Add corbels and other embellishments.

DESIGN 101

True to Style

Staying true to a style involves a little research to ensure a better outcome when building, remodeling, or replacing materials on your home. Although you can mix elements from different styles, a home with a specific architectural type will look better using characteristics typical of its style. A poor blend will skew the facade or merge misplaced details. One material mishap can alter a home's style and turn it into a confusing hodgepodge.

What to **Build**

This restored Queen Anne Victorian has a two-story porch, gable detailing, classic columns, and window styles that are historically accurate. The patterned shape of the roof shingles is repeated within the gable end and dormer wall. The projected two-story bay window is typical of the Queen Anne style and was used to avoid flat wall planes. Other details, such as the ribbon trim that is repeated in the stained glass, express the decorative style of the time.

What **Not** to Build

This neo-Victorian home has elements of the Queen Anne and folk Victorian subtypes, such as the gingerbread ornamentation and spindle work found on the home's porch and gable ends. The second-story bay window is another commonly found detail. However, this modern day rendition lacks some of the basic features of a Victorian composition. The smooth stucco walls are in direct contrast to the wall texture variations typically found on this style house, and the heavy clay tiled roof is also out of context on a Victorian home. Because the basic elements of this style are missing, research would have been helpful before the building process began.

What to **Build**

This asymmetrical restored Queen Anne home features large bay windows. The wood shingles in a variety of shapes and colors are typical of Queen Anne houses. The roof cresting and finials, along with the gable detailing, are also components of true Victorian homes.

Fine-Tuning a Tudor

This medieval Tudor comes very close to historical accuracy, but there are a few problems that need attention. The protruding dormer above the bay window dominates the facade and conflicts with the style of dormer on the other side of the entry. Window styles and shapes are erratic and upset the balance of the elevation.

The window panes across the second story lack consistency.

✓ Standardize window designs and trim treatments.

This dormer is too large.

✓ Decrease the size of the dormer; match the style of the dormer on the left.

What **Not** to Build

The roof and timbers are out of place.

✓ Remove the clutter between the entry and chimney.

The lamps disrupt the stone entry surround.

✓ Remove the lamps and provide lighting inside the entry.

What to **Build**

The corrections to this neo-eclectic Tudor give it a better sense of balance and proportion. The consistent diamond window pattern throughout the second story unifies the elevation. Removing the clutter between the entry and chimney brings attention back to the front door and improves the visual flow on the left side of the home. Changing the dormer on the right so that it matches the one on the left unifies the design and provides balance to the elevation.

Architect's
Notebook

ALL UPPER WINDOWS DIAMOND PATTERN

CHANGE DORMER TO WALL DORMER WITH STONE SURROUND

CHANGE ROUNDED WINDOW TO RECTANGULAR

REMOVE ROOF AND TIMBERS

REMOVE LAMPS

The French Craftsman

The French eclectic dormers are out of place on this obviously Craftsman style home. The curves on the windows and dormer roof conflict with the straight lines found elsewhere on the elevation.

✓ What to Build

The roof on this home is perfectly suited for a shed dormer with exposed rafters. This house now reflects an appropriate modern day interpretation of the Craftsman style.

French eclectic dormers are out of place on this house.

✓ Replace dormers with appropriate shed dormers.

What Not to Build

DESIGN 101

Form Follows Fashion

The neo-eclectic architectural style emerged in the '60s, gained popularity in the '70s, and is still constructed today. It developed as a backlash to the modern and minimalist designs of the '50s and '60s. By definition, neo-eclectic designs plagiarize previous styles by indiscriminately incorporating elements of a previous style into the current housing designs.

In many houses, the materials and architectural elements are often slapped together in an ad hoc fashion, as though the builder visited a housing parts factory and grabbed whatever happened to be on special. The result is a yearning for past traditions, but with a lack of expertise and commitment to spending the time to get it right.

Currently, the influence architects have on residential design is waning. What is unique about our times is who sets the design trends. In the preceding 200 years, public buildings or landmark houses inspired design ideas that were applied to more modest homes. Today, homeowners and builders are playing a more active role in the design of homes. The end result is a form-follows-fashion mentality; designs are influenced by fad rather than historical accuracy.

The simple lines of this modern-style brick home are violated by the gothic-shaped windows. Typical to the neo-eclectic style, the insertion of an inappropriate shape causes issues of scale, proportion, and balance evident on this elevation.

As the neo-eclectic style becomes the rage, various regional substyles begin to dominate the housing market. Neo-Colonial subdivisions in New England, neo-Mediterranean in Florida, and neo-Spanish in the Southwest are examples of this. Although there is stylistic emphasis on the past, the attention to details and composition that were once the requirement of good design are lost among the infestation of "architectural cancer" spreading across the built environment.

DESIGN 101

The Good, the Bad, and the Really Bad

Contemporary View

The clean lines and lack of ornamentation shown here are consistent with contemporary architecture. The transition of the stone and stucco creates a beltline and then challenges us by placing windows that engage that line to create interest. An extremely thin metal awning enhances the entry hierarchy and provides a minimal welcome respite from weather. The contrast of textures and focused composition help the facade avoid the dominant wall monotony that can occur with a shallow-pitched roof.

- The window placement engages the beltline, providing design interest to offset the dominant wall.

- The awning creates a shadow line and entry hierarchy.

- There is minimal detailing.

- Contrasting materials create interest.

A Pleasant Mix of Styles

This is a good example of the difficulties sometimes encountered when trying to place a house within a specific architectural style. With this house, the cornice with dentil moldings is Georgian, the double-hung windows with six pane sashes are Adams, and the entry cover supported by pilasters or columns is Colonial Revival. By using elements with the correct balance, scale, and proportions, several styles can work together on an elevation. The windows are correctly scaled for the first and second levels on this symmetrically balanced home.

- The elevation is symmetrically balanced.

- The windows are scaled proportionately to the implied floor levels.

- Entry elements show Colonial Revival influences.

All Mixed-Up

Neo-Tudor, French eclectic, and Texas territorial are all represented on this facade, and they are combined in a way that ignores balance, proportion, massing, and any remote sense of design logic. The result is the ineffectual composition of a hybrid facade.

- Three styles are represented here. The false aging of the wall represents the neo-Tudor style; the tower is French Eclectic; and the metal roof is Texas Territorial.

Classic Blunder

The shape of this home and the hipped roof suggest Greek Revival, and the composite column capitals suggest a Classical Revival design. In this case, the stylistic flaw is in the material application. The scale of the ashlar stone on the wall has a rustic connotation that conflicts with the refinement of the classical column and the entablature above. Changing the stone to a traditional brick would directly affect the aesthetic perception of the design, regardless of style.

- Stone clashes with the classical elements of the entry, columns, and entablature.

Inattention to Detail

In architecture, success is about attention to details when it comes to achieving an aesthetically pleasing design and accurately reflecting a particular style. Although the basics of the Monterrey style are evident, the fine metalwork railings and balcony do not fit within the context of this home. The shutters on the lower level are attempting to cover a triplicate window that is also out of context for a style that calls for paired windows. The roof should be either shake or tile to reinforce the rustic nature of this style.

- The roof should be covered with a material with a rustic texture, such as wood shakes or clay tile.

- Windows rather than doors open onto this false balcony.

- The shutters would not cover the windows when closed.

DESIGN 101

Elements of Style

Today's eclectic homes have combinations of several different styles. Architectural elements give visual clues that help you trace the influence of a design — important information to have when you remodel your home. Although the homes may not fit perfectly into a pure style, the examples given here have strong details that relate to a dominant type. By reviewing the elevations and looking for the architectural clues, you will familiarize yourself with the identifying features that make up the homes of American neighborhoods.

The low-pitched gable roof and two-story wraparound porch are clues that point to the Greek Revival style. Columns surround the rectangular block that forms the primary mass of the house. The windows have lintels and wooden frames, and the solid white walls accentuated with dark shutters are all identifying features of this style.

The Craftsman style is often referred to as the workman's bungalow. The side-gabled roof, with a centered gable dormer and exposed rafters, is a feature of this subtype. All the elements, including the columns with battered sides, the full-width porch, and windows with multipane upper sashes, are classic features of this style. Even the muted earth tones reflect the use of natural materials commonly found on Craftsman homes.

This home follows the Greek Revival cottage subtype. It has wood siding and a full-length porch. The pediment dormers have dentil molding that is repeated in the entablature.

The Spanish influence can be seen in the low-pitched, side-gabled, red clay roof that extends to the arched openings along the porch. Ornate doors and wooden-framed windows are commonly used on Spanish Eclectic homes.

The modernistic American Deco style home has a boxy mass with a flat roof, single-pane windows, and industrial doors. The smooth, unadorned wall surfaces are usually white, as seen here.

Tudor-style homes, like this one, feature multiple materials with mixed patterns and several gables. Wooden timbers filled in with stucco and patterned brick in the same plane are common features of this style. Tabs of cut stone surrounding an arched entry are another identifying clue.

The broken pediment above the door and the two-story columns are clues that this home is Neoclassical. A roof balustrade, full-length first-story rectangular windows, and dentil molding are also traits of this style.

CHAPTER 12

360-Degree Architecture

Wrapped in Good Design

Good design should not stop at the front elevation of the house; it applies to the entire facade. Unfortunately, with today's emphasis on the floor plan, the back and sides of many houses appear to be an afterthought. Homes that look perfect from the front often lose their credibility once you turn the corner. We are finding blank walls without landscaping, irregular window placement, and material mayhem among the new residences that line our streets. These disasters are particularly bothersome on corner lots where three sides of the house are visible from the street.

In today's building environment the fast-food generation is becoming the fast-house generation. Often times the architectural principles of mass, balance, scale, and proportion are not applied to all sides of the house plans during the design phase. If the initial plans incorporate these principles, the sides and back will be a reflection of what is found on the front, regardless of how quickly a house is constructed.

The materials and design on the side and back of a home do not necessarily have to mirror the front, but if they change, they should change only with purpose. Carrying a theme or element to all sides creates a seamless design that can be appreciated from any angle. If the elevation is photographed on all sides and the photos are placed next to one another, they should appear as though they belong together. Having a great front elevation without applying the same design logic to the sides is like turning in a term paper with a great cover sheet but an inadequate stack of papers behind it. Some elements of good 360-degree architecture include

- The design principles of scale, mass, balance, and proportion, which are as important on the sides and rear of a house as they are on the front.

- Materials used on the rear and sides of a house that match or complement those found on the front of the house.

✓ What to Build

The rear view of this house extends its architectural theme. The back porch and extensive landscaping add to the outdoor living space. The pair of chimneys anchors the projecting wings and frames the central facade. The low shrubbery shows off the architecture. Here we have a home that looks just as nice from the back as it does from the front.

✓ What to Build

The distinctive design of this house is carried from the front to the sides and rear. Details such as the shape of the siding, window styles, and color scheme remain the same no matter which side of the house is viewed.

What **Not** to Build

What to **Build**

This home ignores design principles used on the side facing the street. The horizontal wood siding visually lengthens an already elongated wall. Adding windows, or at least landscaping, would help balance this side of the house.

This rear view includes the details of this home's Spanish Eclectic style. The covered porch serves as an outside living area. The iron railings on the open balconies and the chimney treatment are consistent with the home's style.

Window-Poor Design

This large home is sprinkled with windows that are too small and too few. In addition, the windows that are there have been placed haphazardly and lack any sense of design interest. The two monolithic garage doors seem out of place. The view shown here is from the street, illustrating the importance of 360-degree architecture.

The windows are too small and too few.

Add more windows to enhance the wall.

The roofing material does not complement the stone walls.

Metal roofing is a better choice for this house.

What Not to Build

A new entry element creates interest.

Supplement new windows with appropriate ornamentation.

✔ What to **Build**

This large home now has the appropriate number and size of windows needed to interrupt the expansive stone. Wooden shutters bring life to the windows by adding a contrasting color. The clean-lined metal roof puts the emphasis back on the home below. The new garage doors and the new entry design enhance the entire elevation. The end result is a facade that is wrapped with good design principles.

Architect's Notebook

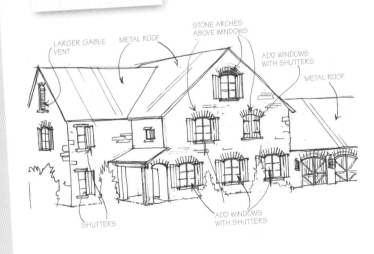

LARGER GABLE VENT

METAL ROOF

STONE ARCHES ABOVE WINDOWS

ADD WINDOWS WITH SHUTTERS

METAL ROOF

SHUTTERS

ADD WINDOWS WITH SHUTTERS

Lack of Detail

The rear view of this home does not apply the same detail that is found on the front elevation. The roof eaves do not line up on the first or second levels, which creates a lack of continuity along the roof mass. The monotonous windows and doors do nothing to take away the focus from the rambling chaotic roof.

The painted half timbers are a failed attempt at detail.

✓ Remove timbers.

What **Not** to Build

There are numerous bland windows and doors.

✓ Add multipaned windows for interest.

The roof eaves do not line up.

✓ Create continuous eaves

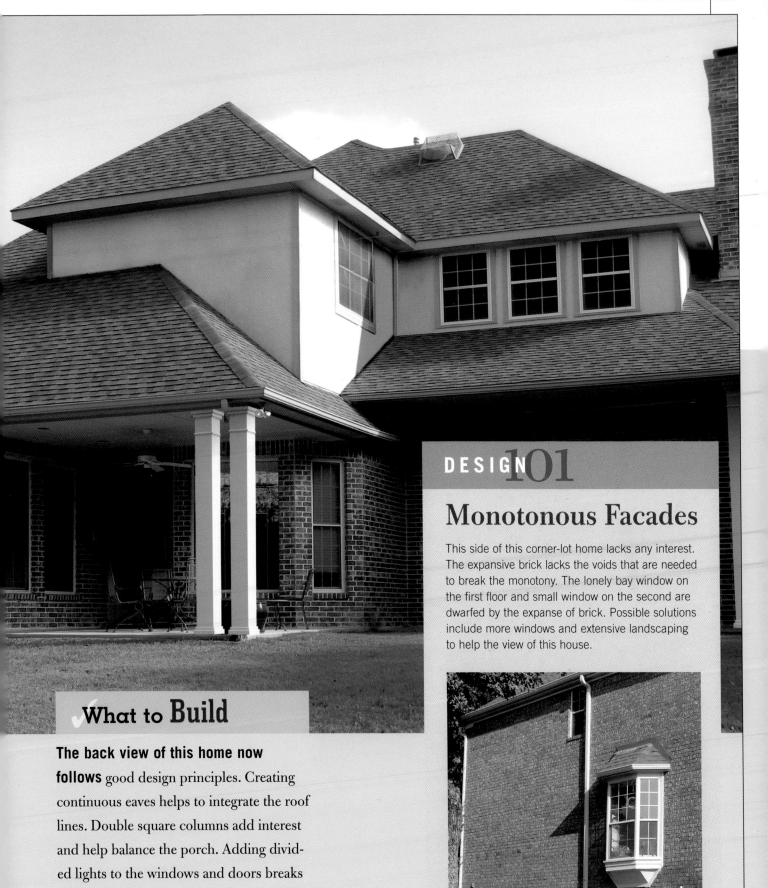

DESIGN 101

Monotonous Facades

This side of this corner-lot home lacks any interest. The expansive brick lacks the voids that are needed to break the monotony. The lonely bay window on the first floor and small window on the second are dwarfed by the expanse of brick. Possible solutions include more windows and extensive landscaping to help the view of this house.

✔ What to Build

The back view of this home now follows good design principles. Creating continuous eaves helps to integrate the roof lines. Double square columns add interest and help balance the porch. Adding divided lights to the windows and doors breaks up the monotony across the back.

CHAPTER 13

Landscaping

Living Architecture

The fundamental principles of balance, mass, rhythm, scale, and proportion that contribute to aesthetically pleasing elevations also apply to landscaping. The organization of trees, shrubs, ground cover, walls, walkways, fences, and other elements that make up the outdoor environment can enhance or detract from a home's appearance.

Much like the architecture of a home, landscaping must follow a sense of order and bring unity to the landscape and elevation. To visually link the elements in a design, repeat them in different areas and locations. A material used on the facade, such as stone, can be repeated in the walls around a patio or used as edging for a plant bed. Plant pots or hanging baskets along a front porch with the same type flowers planted in beds. The order, or "big picture," should have variety. But just as with the exterior elevation, too many competing elements create visual chaos. Ideas for effective landscaping design include

- Repeated elements, such as stone or brick, in different areas of the landscape to unify the design with the elevation.

- Symmetrically designed landscapes that complement a formal architectural style.

- Asymmetrically designed landscapes that work well with a more casual style, such as cottages or Craftsman-style homes.

- Grouping materials of the same type, in groups of three to create a sense of unity. If materials are planted in groups of two, the eye splits the elements apart.

- Creating a design rhythm by repeating elements in the design.

- Gateways that create focal points and are an effective way to establish transitions from one area to another.

- Taking into consideration the mature size of planting material when designing your landscape.

What to Build

The native plant materials complement the Spanish-style architecture. The wrought-iron gate establishes the transition from the outside to the inside of the courtyard.

What Not to Build

The symmetrically balanced landscaping conflicts with the asymmetrically balanced home. The oversized hedges obscure the architectural details. An asymmetrically designed landscape would complement this home and reinforce the pleasing proportions of the facade.

Although the initial size of these accent trees was in scale with the elevation, they are now out of proportion with the home and obscure the architectural details of the home. Taking into consideration the mature size of the trees would have prevented this problem.

This landscaping is in scale with the elevation. However, symmetrical principles would dictate consistent plant types on each side. In this example, the shrubs will bloom at different times of the year, creating a visual imbalance.

DESIGN 101

Outdoor Living Areas

The increased popularity of patios, decks, garden sitting area, pools, and gazebos has carried the living experience outdoors for many homeowners. Both natural and synthetic materials make these areas functional and provide the opportunity to extend design elements on the elevation of the house to the outdoor areas.

This covered porch uses slate flooring that repeats colors used on the walls of the house. The furniture and plants add color, resulting in an inviting area that beckons visitors to sit and relax.

Stepping-stones create a garden path that leads to a secluded garden retreat.

Do's and Don'ts of Landscaping

Don't This bare landscaping is not in proportion to the home. The two-story columns and projecting two-story windows create strong vertical elements that are reinforced by the tall trees in the landscape. Visual weight is needed on the ground to draw your eye back to the entry. The planting beds should be extended with the addition of a tree or taller shrub on the left.

Do The vine emphasizes the curve in the arch detail of the porch. The canopy of the tree mirrors this form.

Don't Although these shrubs are consistently low across the elevation, adding some height at each end of the shrubbery, and extending the plant beds from the entry down the walkway, will create better proportions with the elevation.

Do The symmetrical, formal landscaping suits the architecture of this stately home.

Do The mondo grass intersecting the flagstone walkway creates rhythm and walks your eye to the symmetrically balanced landscaping. The roping in the arch of the entrance is repeated in the spiral topiaries.

Don't A French door is an opportunity to integrate the architecture into the landscaping by opening onto a patio or covered walkway. These French doors lose their prominence and purpose by opening onto an insignificant planting bed.

Do The rhythm of the trellis slats draws your eye to the entrance. The ground cover frames the tranquil walkway.

Do This home is a good example of using color in landscaping to complement the materials used in the home. The flowers repeat the color in the walls, and roof tiles and the proportionately sized pots echo the material in the railing.

Do The variety of plant materials used in this asymmetrically balanced landscaping reflects the cottage feel of the home. The plantings are in proportion to the facade and are not overwhelming.

Continued on next page

Continued from previous page

Do The repeated arches and wooden brackets create rhythm along this courtyard. The ironwork and vines accent the architecture.

Don't The mass of trees in front of this home completely obscures the view from both directions. The entrance is hidden, and the landscaping sends an unwelcoming message to visitors.

Do The hanging ferns and blooms add personality to the corner of this all-American porch. The scale of the greenery allows a view from both sides of the rail.

Do Ponds bring variety and interest to landscaping, providing a tranquil view from inside the home.

Do The entry courtyard divides the public and private spaces. The tree creates a focal point in this outdoor room.

Do Hard surfaces can be interrupted with landscaping to soften the facade. This front drive ends at the stucco wall.

Decorative Landscape Lighting

Landscape lighting extends your outdoor living space long after the sun goes down. The imperfections of daylight are washed away as new moods and forms are created.

Use light to gently wash over the architecture and the landscape around it. The goal is to create natural-looking light with no visible source. Deciding which areas are to be lit is the first step in developing a lighting plan. Pathways and steps, foliage and lawns, dining and living spaces, such as gazebos or pools, are the most common areas. Tips for placing lights include the following:

- To avoid glare, place fixtures as high as possible. Direct the lights so that the source is invisible and only the effect of the lights is seen. Using shielded fixtures that direct the light away from the viewer's eyes also helps to avoid glare.

- The higher the fixture, the larger the light spread on the ground.

- To light the elevation, place light fixtures in trees or other vertical elements to control where light falls on the elevation. If trees are not available, place lights far back at ground level to avoid having the base brighter than the rest of the house.

- Avoid placing lights where the light source is obvious. The viewer should experience a soft glow, not a harsh glare.

Accent lighting creates a warm glow, highlighting the architectural element on the wall.

Up-lighting the tree behind the wall creates drama in the trunk and leaves. The warm light of the interior patio contrasts with the cool light on the foliage. Shadows reflected from the tree form patterns above the arch leading to the patio.

Gently washing plant material evenly with down-lighting creates a natural moonlit environment. The warm light on a dimmer illuminates the steps with a candle-like glow.

Warm light bathes this patio, creating an inviting atmosphere for outdoor living.

Resource Guide

The following list of manufacturers and associations is meant to be a general guide to additional industry and product-related sources. It is not intended as a listing of products and manufacturers represented by the photographs in this book.

Publications

The Elements of Style: An Encyclopedia of Domestic Architectural Detail
Stephen Calloway, General Editor
Elizabeth Cromley, Consultant Editor, Alan Powers, Reviser
New York: Firefly Books, Ltd. 2005

General Resources

The Society for the Preservation of New England Antiquities
141 Cambridge St.
Boston, MA 02114
617-227-3956
www.historicnewengland.org

National Trust for Historic Preservation
1785 Massachusetts Ave., NW
Washington, D.C. 20036
202-588-6000
www.nationaltrust.org

Products

Andersen Windows
100 Fourth Ave. North
Bayport, MN 55003
800-426-4261
www.andersenwindows.com
Manufactures windows and doors, and accessories for them.

Architectural Products by Outwater, LLC
4 Passaic St.
Wood Ridge, NJ 07075
800-835-4400
www.outwater.com
Manufactures various interior and exterior architectural products.

Artcrete
5812 Hwy. 494
Natchitoches, LA 71457
318-379-2000
www.artcrete.com
Manufactures faux brick stenciled concrete.

Atlas Homewares
326 Miral Loma Ave.
Glendale, CA 91204
818-240-3500
www.atlashomewares.com
Manufactures house numbers, door knockers, and doorbells.

Baldwin Hardware Corp.
841 E. Wyomissing Blvd.
Reading, PA 19611
800-566-1986
www.baldwinhardware.com
Manufactures locks and door hardware.

Behr
3400 W. Segerstrom Ave.
Santa Ana, CA 92704
877-237-6158
www.behr.com
Manufactures paint.

Benjamin Moore & Co.
51 Chestnut Ridge Rd.
Montvale, NJ 07645
201-573-9600
www.benjaminmoore.com
Manufactures paint.

Bomanite
232 S. Schnoor Ave.
Madera, CA 93637
559-673-2411
www.bomanite.com
Manufactures architectural concrete paving and flooring material.

BuyPlantationShutters.com
102 Aubrey Dr.
Butler, PA 16001
800-316-9468
www.buyplantationshutters.com
A source for natural and synthetic shutters and shutter hardware.

C & S Distributors, Inc.
1640 Rte. 5
South Windsor, CT 06074
800-842-7307
www.c-sdistributors.com
Provides building supplies for building and remodeling projects.

CAS Design Center

12201 Currency Circle

Forney, TX 75126

800-662-1221

www.casdesign.com

A source for interior and exterior architectural details.

CertainTeed

800-782-8777

www.certainteed.com

Manufactures roofing materials, siding, windows, and fence, deck, and rail components.

Chadsworth's 1-800-Columns

277 North Front St.

Wilmington, NC 28401

800-486-2118

www.columns.com

Manufactures natural and synthetic columns and pillars.

Classic Details

Southern Rose

P.O. Box 280144

Columbia, SC 29228

www.classicdetails.com

Manufactures interior and exterior architectural details for the home.

Clopay Building Products

8585 Duke Blvd.

Mason, OH 45040

www.clopay.com

Manufactures residential garage doors.

Devoe Paint

15885 W. Sprague Rd.

Strongsville, OH 44136

440-297-8635

www.devoepaint.com

Manufactures interior and exterior paint.

Dutch Boy

800-828-5669

www.dutchboy.com

Manufactures interior and exterior paint.

GAF Materials Corp.

1361 Alps Rd.

Wayne, NJ 07470

973-628-3000

www.gaf.com

Manufactures roofing materials.

Garden Supply Co.

1421 Old Apex Rd.

Cary, NC 27513

919-460-7747

www.gardensupplyco.com

A source for plants, including annuals, perennials, trees, and shrubs, and garden complements, such as fountains, statuary, and garden art.

GardenWeb

www.gardenweb.com

Offers seed and plant exchanges, plant reference guides, and links to shopping sites.

Gerkin Windows & Doors

P.O. Box 3203

Sioux City, IA 51102

800-475-5061

www.gerkin.com

Manufactures aluminum windows, storm doors, vinyl windows, and patio doors.

Hooks & Lattice

5671 Palmer Way, Ste. K

Carlsbad, CA 92010

800-896-0978

www.hooksandlattice.com

Manufactures window boxes and planters.

Intermatic, Inc.

Intermatic Plaza

Spring Grove, IL 60081

815-675-7000

www.intermatic.com

Manufactures lighting products, including low-voltage lighting systems.

James Hardie Siding Products

26300 La Alameda, Ste. 250

Mission Viejo, CA 92691

888-542-7343

www.jameshardie.com

Manufactures fiber-cement siding, backerboard, and pipe.

Jeld-Wen, Inc.

P.O. Box 3203

Sioux City, IA 51102

800-535-3936

www.jeld-wen.com

Manufactures windows, exterior doors, patio doors, and garage doors in numerous styles and sizes.

Kestrel Shutters

9 East Race St.

Stowe, PA 19464

800-494-4321

www.diyshutters.com

Manufactures shutters.

Kwikset Corp.

19701 DaVinci

Lake Forest, CA 92610

800-327-5625

www.kwikset.com

Manufactures residential locksets and door hardware.

Marvin Windows and Doors

P.O. Box 100

Warroad, MN 56763

888-537-7828

www.marvin.com

Manufactures windows and swinging and sliding doors.

Monier Lifetile

P.O. Box 19792

Irvine, CA 92623

209-982-1473

www.monierlifetile.com

Manufactures roof tiles of various weights and styles.

Nightscaping

1705 E. Colton Ave.

Redlands, CA 92374

800-544-4840

www.nightscaping.com

Manufactures professional outdoor lighting.

Park Seed Company

1 Parkton Ave.

Greenwood, SC 29647

800-213-0076

www.parkseed.com

Offers plant seeds, bulbs, and gardening supplies.

Pella Windows & Doors

102 Main St.

Pella, IA 50219

www.pella.com

Manufactures windows and exterior doors.

Pratt and Lambert Paints

800-289-7728

www.prattandlambert.com

Manufactures paint.

Restoration Hardware

800-910-9836

www.restorationhardware.com

Manufactures indoor and outdoor furniture, windows, and lighting accessories.

Schlage Lock Co.

1010 Sante Fe St.

Olathe, KS 66051

888-805-9837

www.schlage.com

Manufactures locksets.

Style Solutions, Inc.

960 West Barre Rd.

Archbold, OH 43502

800-446-3040

www.stylesolutionsinc.com

Manufactures interior and exterior architectural details for the home.

Therma-Tru Doors

1750 Indian Wood Circle

Maumee, OH 43537

800-843-7628

www.thermatru.com

Manufactures fiberglass exterior doors.

The Scotts Company

14111 Scottslawn Rd.

Marysville, OH 43041

888-270-3714

www.scotts.com

Offers lawn and garden products.

The Sherwin-Williams Company
101 Prospect Ave., NW
Cleveland, OH 44115
800-4 SHERWIN
www.sherwin-williams.com
Manufactures paint.

Timberlane Woodcrafters, Inc.
197 Wissahickon Ave.
North Wales, PA 19454
800-250-2221
www.timberlane.com
Manufactures exterior wood shutters.

Valspar Corporation
1191 Wheeling Rd.
Wheeling, IL
800-845-9061
www.valspar.com
Manufactures paint.

Weathershield Windows and Doors
One Weather Shield Plaza
Medford, WI 54451
715-748-2100
www.weathershield.com
Manufactures windows and exterior doors.

Agencies & Associations

Energy Star
1200 Pennsylvania Ave., NW
Washington, DC 20460
888-782-7937
www.energystar.gov
Energy Star provides programs and products designed to save energy.

National Association of the Remodeling Industry (NARI)
800-611-NARI
www.nari.org
An organization of contractors, remodelers, subcontractors, and design-build firms that offers education, tips, and a referral service to consumers.

The American Institute of Architects (AIA)
1735 New York Ave., NW
Washington, DC 20006
800-242-3837
www.aia.org
A national professional organization for licensed architects. Local chapters offer a referral service to consumers.

The American Society of Landscape Architects (ASLA)
636 Eye St., NW
Washington, DC 20001
202-898-2444
www.asla.org
A national professional organization of landscape architects.

Architectural Salvage

Old House Journal Restoration Directory
www.oldhousejournal.com
800-234-3797

PreservationWeb
P.O. Box 1329
Vienna, VA 22180
800-707-4330
www.preservationweb.com
Web and print source for regional restoration products and services.

SalvageWeb
www.salvageweb.com
Website provides salvage book recommendations and regional salvage supplier information.

Salvo: Architectural Salvage, Garden Antiques & Reclaimed Building Materials
P.O. Box 333
Cornhill on Tweed
TD 12 4YJ, Northumberland, England
Telephone: +44 1890 820333
www.salvoweb.com
Extensive Web resources and publisher of several print publications.

Glossary

Arbor – a shaded structure covered by vines, branches, flowers, or shrubs on a latticework form.

Arch – a circular or elliptical span.

Architect – a licensed professional who designs structures, such as buildings and homes.

Architrave – the lowest part of a beam or entablature that extends across the top of columns.

Asymmetrical balance – an arrangement of mixed elements such as forms, shapes, colors etc. that are equally distributed on either side of a centerline and create balance through varied weight or visual weight.

Atrium – a garden or courtyard that is surrounded by a structure.

Austin Stone – a light colored stone named after the stone quarries in Austin, Texas

Backlighting (silhouetting) – a method of landscape lighting that places bulbs behind open or lacy foliage to create shadows.

Balance – weight or visual weight of contrasting, opposing, or equal elements that are equal on all sides.

Balustrade – a railing or banister that is often found around porches, balconies, or staircases.

Bargeboard – a decorative board that hangs in a gable and often covers the rafters.

Base – the lowest part of a structure.

Battered column – a column that is wider at the bottom than the top

Bay – a type of window that protrudes from the wall.

Beam – a supporting feature that spans from wall to wall.

Beltline - the horizontal line on an elevation that depicts the first and second stories levels.

Bracket – a structural support that adds strength to a beam.

Cantilevered – a rigid structure or beam projecting horizontally past a supporting post or wall and is supported at only one end.

Capital – the top of a column.

Classical Orders – refers to column types such as Tuscan, Ionic, Doric, Corinthian, and composite.

Clerestory – pronounced *clear story*. A wall of windows found on the upper section of a structure. The clerestory wall is usually above an adjoining roof.

Colonnade – columns found along a covered porch.

Column – an upright pillar or post.

Corbel – a bracket projecting from a wall intended to carry weight.

Cornice – uppermost section of a molding at the top of a wall or just below the roof.

Courtyard – a flat area, usually landscaped, that is surrounded by walls.

Design Logic – the consistent or repetitive use of a theme or element utilized on an elevation or in landscaping.

Dormer – a window which is vertical to the roof and has its own roof, walls, or glazing.

Downlighting (moonlighting) – a landscape lighting technique where the bulbs are attached to a tree or structure to cast light downward.

Eaves – the point of the roof that projects from the wall.

Elevation – the straight on views of a home's exterior.

Entablature – the horizontal mass above columns made up of an architrave, frieze, and cornice.

Facade – the elevation of a structure.

Fanlight – a semicircle window over a window or door.

Fascia – the front of an element or structure.

Faux – something made to resemble something else or a "false" version of something else.

Frieze – a plain or decorative span found in the entablature between the architrave and cornice.

Gable – a triangular-shaped roof.

Gambrel roof – barn-shaped roof.

Gestalt – the perception of the human mind that the whole is more than the sum of its parts.

Glazing – the glass found in windows.

Golden mean – a perfectly proportioned triangle made by extending a squares base line to meet the compass line. Also called the Golden Triangle.

Half-timbered – exposed wood trim in filled with plaster, stone or brick.

Hierarchy – a system of order or importance.

Hightlighting – a lighting technique to accent an architectural element or point of interest.

Hipped – a gabled roof that has slanted or beveled ends.

Integrate – to blend or bring architectural elements together.

Jamb – vertical side of a doorway or window.

Keystone – a central wedge found in the center of an arch.

Le Corbusier – Swiss born French architect known as the Leader of International Style.

Lintel – a load bearing beam found above an opening in a wall.

Loggia – a roofed corridor, balcony, or gallery.

Mansard roof – a roof type that has a near flat upper slope and a steep lower slope, named for architect Francois Mansard (1598 – 1666).

Mass – the larger forms or bulk of a structure.

Masonry – refers to brick or stone held together by a mortar mixture.

Motif – a design that is the predominant theme or pattern.

Molding – decorative pieces, usually wood, found in architecture.

Mullions – a vertical span between windows.

Muntins – wood bars that hold panes of glass in a window.

Order – the underlying framework of a composition.

Oriel – a projecting bay window on an upper floor supported by corbels or stonework.

Parapet – a low wall projecting from a roof, once used as a wall of defense on castles.

Pediment – a triangular portion of a gable end.

Pergola – An arbor with an open roof of rafters supported by posts or columns.

Piazza – a large porch on one or more sides of a home or building.

Pilaster – a flat column projecting out from a wall.

Pitch – refers to the slope of a roofline.

Portico – a covered porch, usually at the entrance, that is supported by columns.

Primary mass – The largest main form of the home.

Proportion – a mathematical relationship of parts to one another or to the whole.

Pythagoras – A Greek philosopher who sought to discover, through musical harmony and geometry, the mathematical principles of reality.

Quatrefoil – a window or opening that has four equal parts and resembles a flower.

Rafter – structural elements that support the roof and extend from the ridge of the roof to the eave.

Rhythm – the patterned repetition or alteration of elements that create the illusion of movement.

Rule of Five – a system which gives points to windows, roof types, and materials.

Rules of Pattern – a set of guidelines devised to prevent "over patterning" of materials.

Quoin – stones that run vertically up the corner of a wall.

Scale – the size relationship of elements judged in relation to a point of reference.

Secondary mass – the secondary forms of a home such as a chimney or entry element.

Shed roof – a roof that slopes in one direction.

Shaft – the middle part of a column.

Spindles – posts within a banister.

Stucco – a cement mixture used as an exterior wall covering.

Symmetrical – mirror image of a structure on both sides of a centerline.

Transom window – a window found above a door or other window.

Truncated – terminated abruptly or cut off at the top.

Unity – the harmonious relationship among elements of an architectural or landscape design.

Uplighting – a landscape lighting technique in which the fixture is placed at the base of an object and light is projected upward.

Veranda – a roofed porch.

Vergeboard – a decorative face board set under the roof edge of a gable.

Vitruvian Man – a famous drawing that was completed in 1490 by Leonardo da Vinci which consists of a man standing with arms and legs spread, and is named after a Roman architect, Vitruvius, who designed temples based on proportions of the human body.

Wall Dormer – a window projecting from the wall at the roofline.

Index

Photo Credits

All Architect's Notebook illustrations by Robby Reid, R.A.
All other illustrations by Clarke Barre
All photography by Dan Piassick unless otherwise noted

pages 12–13: JupiterImages/Creatas images **page 15:**
JupiterImages/ Creatas images **pages 22–23:** courtesy
of Frontgate **pages 40:** both courtesy of JELD-WEN
Windows & Doors **page 41:** top both courtesy of
JELD-WEN Windows & Doors **pages 60–61:** Sandra
Edelman **pages 74–75:** courtesy of Marvin Windows
and Doors **page 76:** courtesy of JELD-WEN Windows
& Doors **page 110:** top both courtesy of Jack Arnold
Companies **page 115:** Sandra Edelman **page 119:** top
right Sandra Edelman **page 121:** Judy Gaman **page
125:** inset, top Judy Gaman **pages 146–147:** Sandra
Edelman **page 188:** both Sandra Edelman **page 189:**
bottom right Judy Gaman **pages 198–199:** Charles
Smith, design: Significant Homes by Douglas Newby
page 201: top John Benoist Pro Photo of Dallas,
design: George Lewis Custom Homes; bottom center
Judy Gaman **pages 202–203:** both Judy Gaman **pages
204–205:** left & top right Sandra Edleman; inset Judy
Gaman **pages 206–207:** John Benoist Pro Photo of
Dallas, design: George Lewis Custom Homes **page
209:** Sandra Edelman **page 210:** top left Sandra
Edelman; center right Judy Gaman; bottom right
Charles Smith, design: Significant Homes by Douglas
Newby **page 212:** top right, bottom right & top left
Judy Gaman **page 213:** all Richard V. Lentz/Lentz
Landscape Lighting

About Dan Piassick BFA

Dan's photography can be seen in numerous maga-
zines and books. He has shot for *Better Homes and
Gardens*; *Trade Secrets*, *Windows and Walls*, *Color
Schemes*, and *Beautiful Baths*, as well as *Trading
Spaces*, *Ladies Home Journal*, *D Magazine* and many
others. His images also grace the pages of many books
on design and architecture throughout the country.

Dan has a degree in fine art photography from
the University of Arizona. His unique ability to use
light is what sets him apart as a photographer. When it
comes time to building his personal residence Dan will
be sure it passes the "What Not to Build" test.

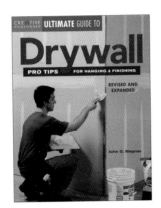

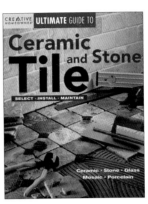
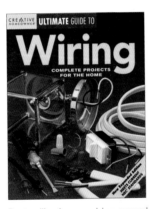
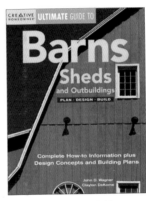
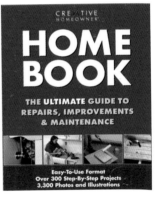

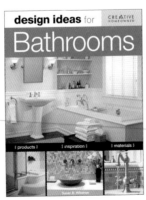